The 12 Steps to Joy and Happiness

Finding the "Kingdom of God that lies within" Luke 17:21

David L. Peters

BALBOA.
PRESS
A DIVISION OF HAY HOUSE

Balboa Press books may be ordered through booksellers or by contacting:

Balboa Press
A Division of Hay House
1663 Liberty Drive
Bloomington, IN 47403
www.balboapress.com
1 (877) 407-4847

Print information available on the last page.

ISBN: 978-1-5043-7641-9 (sc)
ISBN: 978-1-5043-7643-3 (hc)
ISBN: 978-1-5043-7642-6 (e)

Library of Congress Control Number: 2017903711

Balboa Press rev. date: 01/24/2018

Contents

To my wife Eileen. You have shown me the love of God for more than fifty-five years. Even when I tried to ignore that love, you never wavered— you brought me back home to my heart.

To our children: Barbara, Karen, Maureen, Janet, Tim, Dan, and Drew. You have had to put up with my workaholic efforts in everything I did—and you turned out so well despite me.

Introduction

*M*y life has been filled with miracles, time after time, even when I have not lived up to the promise time after time, due to my own weakness. And yet the experiences of life have taught me in ways that no other path of life could have taught me: it is possible to have joy and happiness in great chunks of life even when events should have led to gloom, despair, and hopelessness. The number of synchronicities in my life has astounded me; amazing coincidences have appeared time after time.

Many have considered me extraordinarily lucky. One event that illustrates that type of action was when I graduated from college (University of Dayton) with a degree in electronic engineering (BSEE) in 1959. I had already accepted a PhD offer in the fascinating field of radio astronomy, but I was a bit jealous of my classmates who were traveling here and there for interviews. I had always wanted to visit New York City, so I looked at the list of upcoming companies coming in to interview engineering graduates, and picked the first one that was in New York City, and studied up on the company.

I had an interview, expecting and receiving an invitation to go to New York City for a second interview.

I requested the interview coincide with a weekend and that they let me stay in New York City for the weekend. The request was granted. I flew to New York City, aced the interview, and was offered a job. Of course, I already had the PhD offer. But I really enjoyed myself over the weekend. The company I had interviewed was on Long Island, a neat train ride into the city.

I had always been interested in television electronics, picking up spending money in college by repairing TVs, usually just replacing vacuum tubes (those were the thing in the fifties.) The job offer from the company was to work on FAA displays for the control towers at airports, and I reasoned that it was close to TV. I was a bit older than most graduates (twenty-five) since I had worked before going off to college. When I realized I would have to spend five to seven years getting my advanced degree followed by a few more years with post-degree effort, I took the job in the New York City area.

A couple months after accepting the offer—while I was still waiting to graduate—I helped out at an electronics trade show at my school. I was a 'gofer' and helped vendors with whatever they needed. A vendor asked me what I was doing after graduation, and I told him. He casually mentioned that the company I had joined also had a small television-research group that included many of the inventors of commercial television.

I called and asked about the group, but I was told that they were very small. There were fewer than fifteen people, and they only accepted people with at least fifteen years of experience in television electronics. I thought it would be a goal to work there in the future, and I went on to graduate a few weeks later.

When I arrived for my first day on the job after driving seven hundred miles, I was asked if I was still interested in working at the research center. The research group had put a request in the *preceding Friday* for a recent college graduate who they could train. Since I had asked about the group, they asked me. I accepted, and it changed my life. I spent ten years there, working for the leading television experts. The vice president of the operation, Bernard D. Loughlin, was known as the "grandfather of color TV." He had 120 patents, including the basic patent on the color encoding used today in television broadcasts and receivers in the United States.

I learned so much about how the human eye operates, how television fools the brain into thinking everything is continuous, what color is, and how the brain uses color information. It led to a career in the flight-simulation industry and the subsequent founding of my own company with a partner in that industry. In 2015, I "retired" (one never retires when you own a business) at the age of eighty to pursue writing.

That is just one example out of many synchronicities that have dotted my life. Most just call me lucky, but I do not consider it luck. It has been the result of a conscious relying on the grace of God in my life—since childhood (except for a few years in my teens when I wrestled with the concept of God). I emerged from my teens with a more mature concept than the blind faith of a child.

My conceptual knowledge of God has changed dramatically over the decades. It is still in a state of flux as more knowledge is poured into my life and I experience God in my everyday life.

I was born and raised a Roman Catholic, and I went through sixteen years of Catholic education. I still attend a Catholic church with my wife, and I am a member of one of the few—if not the only—progressive parishes in our diocese. I have been actively leading groups for most of the past fifty years. I spent fifteen years establishing and leading (on the diocesan level) a group known as the Cursillo Movement. This lay-directed group is interested in bringing the teachings of Jesus into the everyday work environments and creating more just working environments in our world.

I also worked in groups with, and used, the Alcoholics Anonymous (AA) twelve-step program to guide my life when things seemed a bit rough (to put it mildly). The teaching steps in this book are a direct result of those life-saving steps.

I go to church with my wife of fifty-six years. My personal beliefs are somewhat different than the mainline Catholic teachings and most mainline Christian teachings. I watch little television, and I have watched little television throughout my life. I prefer to read or write in the time I have left for this pass through the world of physicality. Many of my beliefs are connected to science, especially quantum physics (the science of the very small) and the cosmos and its breathtaking implications of life (now and eternal). My writings and teachings center around the unity of God and the universe; no true knowledge of both can have contradictions, that is, true theology and true science must arrive at the same conclusion.

The second most important set of study I have recently taken is the Conversation with God series of books. In them, God talked through the pen of Neale Donald Walsch about how the "God System" really works in our lives and the life of the universe and beyond. I arrived at most of the key teachings in the books on my own. I was "directed" to pick up the first book of the nine-book series. I have no other term I can use. I could not refuse this directive. My arm moved of its own volition to pick up the book when I had no idea what it was. Neale Donald Walsch wrote the series in conjunction with God. I facilitate a group that studies the books of the series, and we meet every Thursday evening. Do I believe all that I read in these books? The answer is no, but I do follow the vast majority of what I read in this series.

I use many quotes from the Christian Bible since that is the faith I have studied for more than seventy years. I read the Bible, cover to cover, starting with Genesis, in eighth grade. While I have read other sacred texts over the years, I still find that the Bible, especially the words of Jesus, is the most powerful way to express the truths of the universe.

There is no set series of beliefs required to follow this book, except an acceptance of some type of 'higher power' that exists beyond oneself. The 'higher power' can be of any form, and I generally call that power 'God' or a similar title. You can use any title you feel comfortable using for your 'higher power'.

I consider myself a follower of Jesus. His living presence was filled with the grace of his Father/Mother, that eternal force we call God, the Creator of all, and the being of all throughout the infinity of all. There are no words to express this being. All terms we use are limited in concept so that we can have some vague understanding of what is meant. Only in the obscure math of quantum physics are some of these outer limitless expressions presented. Even those arriving at the math cannot explain them to themselves. They just give vague thoughts about their meaning. If the concepts expressed by the math are looked at from the direction of the infinity of God, they start to make sense.

I have been in the presence of God in my life. I will talk about that later. But that experience 50 years ago changed my life profoundly, as I went from having faith in God to knowing God, through direct experience. Only through personal experience can we move to that level of understanding Jesus's words *"The Kingdom of God lies within."* (Luke 17:21, KJV)

Some of the theology expressed in this treatise may seem startling, but they have a long history. I am a firm believer in 'pen*en*theism', which is *not* 'pantheism'. 'Pantheism' is the belief that all of nature is God, and only nature; that God does not exist outside of the material world. 'Pan*en*theism' is the statement that God includes all of nature, that nature rests in God, but God is much more. In other words, God is truly the All in All. Perhaps the most prominent saint in the past who taught that was St. Francis of Assisi. St. Francis called the earth brother earth, talked and sang to the animals, who according to legend came up close to him, for he recognized the God within their beings. So don't be surprised when I speak of the All in All as being God, which includes the energy fields that we call matter. St. Paul put it: *"So that God may be all in all."* (1 Corinthians 15:28, NIV) and *"But Christ is all, and is in all."* (Colossians 3:11, NIV).

God has been part of my life more than eighty years, including my earliest memories. I am always amazed when I comment about this nature and people look at me like I am crazy. It was many years before I understood that this type of relationship with the Almighty Spirit is rare—even among those who have dedicated their lives to serve God. I have had this sense of the presence all my life, and I assumed everybody did. I found out that I was very wrong. Most people have no sense of the overwhelming Spirit that has guided me all my life. They are winging it. I have struggled to help others find the way to this comforting and wonderful level of understanding, and I have been disappointed that most people I have talked with had no way to see the possibilities.

Thus, this book was born. We will walk with the aid of thirty-nine meditations along a path I have walked for eighty years. I hope a few—even if only one—will find the wonderful sense of completeness that I have. If that occurs, all is worth the effort to put this concept and program out in the world. Even if no one picks it up, I have done what God has been pushing me to do for the past few years. This treatise is one of the reasons I have been on this path on earth—with all its pain and all its glory.

This is a book of meditations along a path to experience the living God. There are many ways to use this book. One way is to read it through and then read it one meditation at a time. Spend time on each concept—but no more than one meditation a day. Do not be afraid to spend more than one day on a meditation. That time cements a path into your mental framework, and the use of these specific meditations will lead you far on the path. I ask questions at the end of each chapter, and I strongly recommend that you keep a personal journal to answer these questions, so that you can see for yourself how your thinking moves along.

So welcome to the journey of a lifetime. It is only a start—as you will see.

Chapter 1

Abundance

So God created humanity in God's own image; in the image of God, God created them. Male and female God created them.
—Genesis 1:27, NIV

*P*rosperity has become a favorite word of some of contemporary, self-empowering speakers and preachers. *The Secret* is a book about how to become rich and comfortable only by thinking about it. The book has led to gatherings that feature a large number of speakers, large crowds, and much hype.

Many mega-churches teach the "prosperity gospel," which is the belief that following the gospels can lead to wealth, prosperity, good health, great jobs, and great cars and homes. If people lose their jobs, have health problems, or suffer other calamities, then they obviously failed in their beliefs. They are told to firm up their faith, and all will be well. If all is not well, they are asked to leave since they obviously do not have faith. They might contaminate others (or, more importantly, reduce the cash flow of the church).

The 'law of attraction' suggests that we attract the world and environment we live in. By thinking, writing lists, and believing firmly, we can change our lives for the better. This term is closer to what I call *abundance*, but it is still used too often in a manner that is very close to *prosperity*.

Many people have been attracted to these messages, and they follow them with great enthusiasm. However, most people find that they fail eventually in their basic message. Life eventually offers challenges that the approaches cannot respond to in any manner that would signal prosperity.

This rubbish has caused most mainstream believers to doubt the very concept that our beliefs and working with God can lead to a good life. I will not use the terms *prosperity* or *attraction*, with their materialistic connotations. Instead, I will use the word *abundance* to form the path of knowing that all is good, no matter what the outward appearance seems to say, and we can live in abundance—filled with joy and happiness—if we so choose.

I have been blessed with abundance.

I have been blessed with physical abundance that has let me live comfortably all of my life, but I have found that the words espoused by those preachers and writers talking about prosperity or attraction have missed the mark of the truth of abundance as I see it. Yes, there is such a thing as abundance, but it requires so much more than wishing for some particular success (i.e., a promotion) and hoping it (the promotion) will occur.

Abundance is real. It is based on the truth that we create our own lives by what we think and do—consciously and subconsciously. The subconscious mind almost always directs our lives, based upon our actions or reactions to the events in our lives. Wishes of the mental or spoken kind by themselves will not become reality, but our thoughts, actions, and patterns of life that lead to that moment of life spell out what the next moment will be. Wishes are just wishes. The fundamental grasp of life we hold spells out the next moment of truth for us—moment by moment.

Our beliefs, understanding, and perspectives create our lives, and if we wish to live in abundance, we adjust our beliefs, understanding, and perspectives to achieve that level of perspective. We shall see that both from the metaphysical viewpoint and the scientific viewpoint our life is a product of our beliefs, understandings, and perspective as one event leads to the next event. This is one of the great truths of life that science is just grasping, and it is causing a giant ripple in thought, especially among those who study the fundamental causes of all that is. Physicists in the quantum physics world have some mighty strange conclusions based on the mathematical theories that

3

seem to hold against the patterns of nature of the very small particles and their extreme energy.

Did I know that I was living a life of abundance at the time? Not really. I understood that life seemed good, that I had a lot of extraordinary good luck, and that my faith in God seemed to be part of the equation. However, it is only from looking back on my more than eighty years of life that I have realized how blessed I have been. I have lived a life of abundance. I have been a "seeker of the kingdom of God," and "all else has been granted me."

As Jesus said, *"Seek first the kingdom of God, and all else will be granted you"* (Matt. 6:33, ESV, modified).

Did I understand what I was doing in this process? No, I did not—but it still happened. There were times when parts of my life were far from that center, but I continued as best I could to "seek the kingdom of God." God continued to grant me all I needed for a good life. Deep in my heart, I held to the God-given truth of the joy and love of God.

We will look at these areas in further detail later, but right now, it is important to see that all we think and do—the patterns we let our minds follow—form the links that set up our lives, step by step. One step leads to the next, and a life of abundance is based upon having a sequence of steps that follow general patterns. These include certain beliefs, understanding, trust in our beliefs and understanding, and firmness in following where they lead—even if the present moment seems far less than desired.

Our thinking sets the course of life.

Our basic thinking patterns form the basis of what occurs in our lives. Are we vague or clear in our thinking? Are we facing things in a negative or positive manner? Is our perspective on life one of passivity, excitement, joy, or gloom? Those characteristics form the basis of our lives, and our lives will unfold according to those directives we put in place in our basic understanding of life.

When we wish for something, we get a wish—not a truth. A wish, by its very nature, states that it is something we do not have. It is only a maybe; it is not a concrete event. The writers of that nature insist in many stories that just by wishing—or 'believing'—we can gain wealth and prosperity in this life. We will rise over all others in the process. Almost all who attend these conferences, and they attend by the thousands, hope to be able to forego illness, become wealthy, and not have to work—just by believing they will do so. They use chants, self-hypnotism, and other techniques to convince themselves it is as they wish. Unfortunately, deep in their being, they do *not* believe. Eventually all that effort is swallowed by events, and it vanishes.

Seek first the kingdom of God, and all else will be granted you.
—Matthew 6:33

I hate to prick the balloon, but it ain't so. Some positive attitude will help, but it will not create wealth (except for those giving the speeches and writing the books). The truth of gaining abundance is not just wishing. It is far more than that. Wishing will only give you the wish. By wishing, you are stating that you do not have abundance. But by approaching abundance from the vista of being one with God, the Eternal Wisdom, the truth of abundance appears. When we are united with God, we see that abundance is granted with respect for our love of others. Love lights the path to help others on their way,

Jesus said, *"Seek first the kingdom of God, and all else will be granted you"* (Matt. 6:33).

When we seek first the kingdom of God and all that it entails, we will be surprised to see that we will have food on the table, sufficient clothes, etc. We may not be wealthy, but we will have everything we need to live abundantly. We will be happy and fulfilled. We will have a place in life that means something to someone—if only to ourselves.

I have lived an abundant life. I always found just the right opportunity before me, and I always took it. It often started out by what many would say was a negative (job loss, etc.), but the result became the nexus of the next phase of my life. I have always expected God to provide the next opportunity at the appropriate moment, and the Eternal Wisdom did just that.

I seldom recognized the moment as a gift from God when it came, but I always responded in a manner that seemed appropriate. As a risk-taker in life, I always went for the gold. Maybe I only ended up with what appeared to be the silver, but I gained knowledge and the skills to continue on the path before me. In hindsight, the silver I saw at that time was the gold.

Abundance is trust in the Creator.

Abundance is the result of total trust in God. No doubt. God will give me all I need. That is the secret. Not self-confidence, or self-will, but trust. Nothing but trust. Not that God would grant me this or that. I trust that God will do the best thing I need at that moment in the eternal now—in this time and space. That level of trust in God becomes knowing. I know that God will give me all I need to be happy.

I accept that we make the future and our lives, and I believe God is the source and fountain of life. God will give me the best there is for me for this moment in time and eternity. All of life is a spontaneous eruption of Creation—never seen before and never to be seen again. It is based on the events of life up to that moment, our reaction to those events, and our vision of the future, leading to the next event. It is usually subconsciously directed.

Only masters like Jesus could consciously direct the events of the future. Even Jesus was tied to the constraints of the life he was leading. He knew the approach he was leading would result in his death, but he accepted his death for the greater good he could sense in the future. He trusted God the Father/Mother and the flow of the Spirit that this was the path to

7

yield the greatest good. Looking at the evolution of humanity, the timing of the presence of Jesus was perfect. It illustrated for us the perfect trust he had in the eternal wisdom to lead humanity to the next step in creative thinking. He knew that each step, while appearing small or even negative, would lead to a change in the patterns of life on the planet.

Even in death, Jesus trusted God.

Even the death of Jesus was a result of the trust of Jesus in the eternal wisdom. He had to trust that his death would result in something that would somehow carry a large part of humanity into the future. It would give humanity a stronger glimpse into the being of God, the Eternal Power who called Itself love, only love.

Jesus understood that humanity was on an evolving platform, and that platform would eventually lead to the setting and growth to paradise. His actions were a step toward that evolving humanity. Today, we are at another cusp. We will move to the next level of evolution or devolve and start again.

Jesus understood that all that he did was a pattern for the future, leading to paths of abundance for billions on the planet. He understood his mission was far more than just the small group that followed him at that time. He had glimpses of the future where his presence was made manifest to the world. Jesus was the living embodiment of the Christ in a form like ourselves, humanity, that spelled out the Divine Love that is the essence of creation. Thus we have Jesus, the Christ, or more commonly, Jesus Christ.

Thus, for Jesus, abundance meant something very different than it means for you or me. It is critical to see that the term carries a wide spectrum of meaning. For Jesus, who lived in the ever presence of his Father, abundance meant something that would arise from his death, perhaps requiring his death to achieve. For you and me, abundance usually means that we have sufficient unto the day—and sometimes a little more. We do not have the trust level of Jesus, and we would perhaps balk at being asked for that level of trust. I will be expanding on the meaning of abundance to mean that we can find joy and happiness in life—no matter want life hands us.

Did Jesus have knowledge that billions would follow him? Probably not. Those numbers could not even be thought of when Jesus walked the world. A number that large did not exist. Jesus was a product of his times. Tens of thousands was as big as there was. He certainly was not schooled in the general schools of the Roman Empire. The local Hebrew schools schooled him, probably until he was in his teens. Jesus may have sought out further studies with the Essenes, or as some stories have it, in the East, such as India. After all he was thirty when he started his mission. Then he was called "Rabbi," or 'learned one'.

I am sure Jesus understood he had a mission greater than just that small piece of land. If not before his death, then after his death, all would have been made clear. The call went to Saint Paul to spread the Word outside that small provincial area where Jesus lived and taught.

Abundance: To Have Sufficient for the Day and More

I have been granted sufficient for the day and more, much to my surprise. I had expected that late in life I would be happy and not have to worry about the basics in life. I have achieved far more. I have, most importantly, the love of my soul mate. God gave that gift to me over fifty-five years ago. I am surrounded by natural beauty that takes my breath away every day. I have sufficient income to enjoy life abundantly and share abundantly with others inside the family and outside. Good health allows me to share my gratitude with others. In addition, I have been granted the knowing that God resides within and without me, enveloping every particle of my being, and joining me to everything in this universe. What more could I ask of life? This is abundance.

My abundance did not fall out of the sky. It came from a willingness to invest in the future. Now that I am past eighty, I have withdrawn from day-to-day leading of my company in its technical direction. I have worked for the past several years to let others lead the way, and I have been blessed by the presence of others with extraordinary capabilities. They are eager to step in. Even in the ordinary work environment, I see the hand of God guiding and providing opportunities for others I trust to lead the work environment in a positive direction. I still find the work in science enthralling, and I see the hand of God in all that I do. It was the correct time to move into the next phase of my life.

Abundance is a way of looking at life. Leading an abundant life does not necessarily mean that one is wealthy in things of this world. It means that one has sufficient abundance to live a full life that feeds the soul, is filled with love, and is filled with things that one loves. Abundance follows trust in the eternal wisdom that all will be good, that all *is* good, and that nothing can break the love that fills me as a part of the Eternal Being. *"So God created humanity in God's own image; in the image of God, God created them. Male and female God created them"* (Genesis 1:27). What a breathtaking statement.

> **Yesterday I was clever,**
> **So I wanted to change the world.**
> **Today I am wise,**
> **So I am changing myself.**
> **—Rumi**

Questions to Ponder

How does the statement in Genesis "Then God said: Let us make humanity in our image, in our likeness—" resound in your soul?

Write down in your journal the ways that you could be an image of God.

You think; therefore you are. Write that down.

You are; therefore you think. How does that twist on the well-known phrase hit you?

You can see beauty and experience joy. Write that down.

Does a life of abundance seem like a dream or could it be a reality in your life?

Take a moment to write down a list of the items you can be thankful about.

You have life. Write that down.

Do you have food on the table? Write that down.

Do you have shelter? Write that down.

Are you reasonably healthy? Write that down.

What more can you be thankful for?

You understand the process, and you will be surprised by how many things you can add to the list.

Meditation

My Eternal Wisdom, the One Who knows me more than I know myself, I look at my life in wonder and gratitude that I have been given so abundantly all that

I have. You have surrounded me with beauty, vibrant life, long life, a partner who knows me better than I know myself, a loving family who inspires me, and sufficient comfort. I can say, "All is well!" All this has happened while you have kept me busy doing tasks, because you have permitted me to expect the best to happen and accept that all that happened has been the best for all concerned. You have helped me understand the power of love, the power of faith and belief, and the power of life. I know that I will be granted enough time to achieve the next step and then the next step in life, one step at a time. I understand and am grateful for the gift of understanding that you and I are one being—in a life that never ends.

Chapter 2

Our Lives Are Ours to Create

"The kingdom of God is not coming with signs to be observed. Neither shall they say, "It is here" or "It is there," for the kingdom of God is within you."
—Luke 17:20-21, English Revised Version, paraphrased

*I*n the last chapter, I hinted that we have the ability to not just affect our lives but to create a totally different experience of our lives. Our very existence is an example of that creative process. We have chosen this life, the experiences we potentially will have, and our purposes in life, on a subconscious level that we seldom understand.

We usually create our lives unconsciously. Do we have the capacity to create our lives consciously if we wish to do so? What power gives us the capability to create our lives unconsciously or consciously? How is this a truth when we see our lives spinning out of control, seemingly in total disregard of our wishes or desires?

To understand why this is the so, we need to understand who we are. This ties in closely with Jesus's words about his miracles and power. *"Greater things than this shall you do"* (John 14:12, ESV). How is this possible? What innate power do we possess to create our own life experiences? The answers to these questions reveal the potential each of us retain—if only we remember who we really are.

We are the image of God.

Neale Donald Walsch's poetic prose sweeps one along to see the beauty of the life we live as part of the core beginnings of what we call God. We are *"heirs of God and coheirs with Christ"* (Romans 8:17, NIV). This is not just an outer cloak we assume. It is part of our core being.

Jesus said, *"That they may be one as we are one—I in them and you in me so that they may be brought to complete unity. Then the world will know that you sent me and have loved them even as you loved me"* (John 17:22–24, NIV)

Jesus stated clearly that God loves us just as God loves Jesus, stating clearly that we are the same as Jesus in the 'senses' of God. These powerful words describe, as many in the early church understood, what Jesus meant when he said, *"Greater things than this shall you do"* (John 14:12, NIV).

The major difference is that Jesus knew exactly who he was: and as such became the living embodiment of the Christ, understanding he was one with God in spirit and in flesh. It is our refusal to accept who we really are that stands as the block to knowing that indeed, we are one in Jesus, one in God.

St. Paul stated that we are equal to Jesus in the eyes of God, "heirs of God and co-heirs with Christ" as spoken by Paul. Jesus said, "Be one as we are one, I in them as you in me." Jesus came to seek us to follow him, to be imitators of him, and to be *one* with him, to be him, the Christ, today—not to worship him. Jesus said, "Follow me." Jesus never said, "Worship me."

Oh Jesus, how far we come from your directives. It is so much easier to worship you than to follow you. In this series of meditations, we will walk the path of following Jesus, seeking to be the body of the Christ, as spoken by Paul in Romans.

After almost eighty years of searching, I understand that we are the very image of God. We understand all that is on a very deep level. Since we are in the very image of God, there is nothing we do not have ingrained into our souls. That portion of our being is the very power (image) of God.

God is the All in All.

We see but a fraction of the power that is God, our Eternal Wisdom, when we view our cosmos. We see only a very small fraction of our cosmos that is visible to our senses. We claim that God is all-powerful. We claim that there is no power outside of God. If a power is outside of God, and God is not that power, then God is not all-powerful. How could that awesome power of our cosmos, a hundred billion galaxies each containing a hundred billion stars, be separate from God? (See the introduction and below for a discussion of the view of St. Francis of Assisi.) Our cosmologists tell us that our universe is filled with real and virtual particles that comprise all possibilities at every moment for that portion of the cosmos. That makes all potential possibilities, no matter how small, still a possibility. This part of physics is the quantum mechanics side of the cosmos. This study has turned our seemingly solid world of classical physics on its head.

Is this how we imagine God is—that all possibilities, no matter how remote, are still possible with God? And how, if all this is separate from God, could all these remote possibilities be possible? If we are totally separate from God, God would have no reason to interfere with the physical world since it is an object different from God. Therefore, the physical world is doing its own thing, irrespective of the fact that God is somewhere.

We cannot have it both ways: either God is totally separate from the physical world and does not intersect with it or God is somehow totally mixed into the physical world. The physical world and God cannot be separated into separate existences, and God is the All in All. Everything is immersed into God – the Christ that has existed in our universe since the start of the universe, the Big Bang.

Quantum physics agrees with the mystics: all is one thing.

For five thousand years, mystics throughout the world—from almost all religions—have claimed that there is only one Supreme Being in the totality of the all. The mystics, including those of the Christian religion, especially in the very early years of Christianity, felt the power throughout their beings to proclaim that humanity existed in Christ's body of the all. What does science say about this concept?

In order to determine the truth, we have to look at what science says about the physical world. It may seem strange to prove how God and the physical world are actually one being. We will use science, which has disdained the suggestion of a God, to see the truth of what we are talking about in this discussion. We will look at some of the findings of quantum physics to understand more deeply the relationship between the physical world and what we call God.

The study of the very small, the world of particle physics and smaller, has shown us that as we explore the ever-smaller quanta, we arrive at stranger and stranger relationships between particles. Particles are the substance of atoms, such as electrons, anti-electrons, quarks, and beyond. As we are all taught in school, all visible matter consists of atoms that are bound together through electrical charges imparted by the arrangement of the electron clouds in the atoms. They bind with other electron clouds to create networks that eventually arrive at what we call matter. They make the world around us that we see, and don't see but can measure.

When we look at atoms, we see a nucleus with a charge and electron clouds circling around to balance out the charge. But if we look at electrons, we see a cloud of energy that never sits still. It is forming and changing at the speed of light to create the illusion of what we call an electron. The atom's nucleus consists of other particles, called quarks of various types, and other strangely named particles that together form the unit we call a nucleus. Deeper looks into the quarks and similar particles reveal energies that create potentials, or relationships, that form the boundaries of the particles that make up quarks. They form other relationships that create atoms and then molecules. Energy of its own is a concept; energy is a nonexistent series of relationships that have attraction and repelling forces that create matter as we know it. Energy has no visible part—no breadth or width or depth—but it is the potential for action only and not a physical reality.

Many physicists say that no physical reality exists. Read that last paragraph again if you need to begin to understand. We will touch on this many times in future chapters. In the end, no physical reality exists. Relationships form units that form more units and end with the universe as we know it. These relationships form the atoms that make our flesh and blood and give rise to the conscious working out that make us, us.

Only relationships (energy) create our universe.

Strange wonders. Nothing exists. There are only relationships that have formed boundaries that create you, me, and all that we love, even life itself, (whatever that is), and the world we see around us.

Is this not an explanation of God?

> *We are what we believe we are.*
> *—Benjamin N. Cardozo*

What else could God be but relationships? *"God is love, only love"* (1 John 4:16, NIV), and at the most fundamental level, our universe, our very being, is love. This is spelled out by relationships that all perceive. We call it matter—rocks, mountains, stars, and people. St. Francis (1181/1182 – 1226), understood perfectly the total interrelationships that are part of the universe. He called that around him "Brother earth, Sister Moon", and spoke with love to the animals, trees, and all around him. Francis saw that hand of God in all living things (animals, plants, as well as humanity) and in all of creation – the earth, moon, and the sun.

The universe we see is the part of God we can see in this limited world of time and limited eyesight. We do not see all of God. We only see the three or four dimensions we can perceive. Some of the theories about the nature of the universe state that our universe has at least ten or eleven dimensions, and we have no idea what exists outside our universe. *"What no eye has seen, what no ear has heard, and what no human mind has conceived"* (1 Corinthians 2:9, NIV) what is present in infinite space and has been churning for eternity.

Even within our universe, we see only about 0.01 percent (or so) of what makes up our known universe. We can only understand dark energy (76 percent) and dark matter (20 percent) from their actions on the movement of the stars and galaxies that we can see since no instrument has detected dark matter or dark energy. Visible matter makes up 4 percent. Visible matter consists of 99 percent interstellar dust, which is too small to be visible, leaving only .01 percent of the universe to make all the glorious cosmos of over 100 billion galaxies, each of which have over 100 billion stars.

If all that we can perceive is some part of God, then it becomes clear that *we* are part of the being or existence we call God. And if we are some part of God, no matter how distantly related, we still have, somewhere within us, the ultimate power of God to be able to do and be all things.

"*Greater things than this shall you do*" (John 14:12, NIV, modified).

"*The kingdom of God lies within*" (Luke 17:21, KJV).

"*In the image of God, God created them*" (Genesis 1:27, NIV).

And if we can do "greater things than this," we have the power to make the hills smooth and the path straight—if we understand and remember all that we are. We have known who and what we are before coming to this plane of existence, but we have forgotten our very being. We only need to remember who and what we are: a being of God, capable of ordering our existence in this or any other plane.

> ***We know what we are***
> ***But not what we may be.***
> ***—William Shakespeare***

Questions to Ponder

Jesus said, "Greater things than this shall you do." Now that science has revealed that we are part of an incredibly large field of energy, how does your existence being much larger than your body affect your thoughts about his words?

Do you think Jesus really meant these words? Can you write down ways that knowledge has led you to understand events in your own life? Write down times that an understanding of a truth has changed your thinking or understanding of another.

How does the potential fact that God is part of the physical world in the energy fields change how you perceive life and the universe?

If God is part of the physical universe, how you would treat the earth differently?

Meditation

My Eternal Wisdom, I bow in gratitude for the understanding you have granted me in this time and space. You have granted me wisdom that once would have been that of the gods, beyond human ken, but is now part of my daily life. I ask that you give me the further wisdom to understand that knowledge as knowledge of You, the Eternal Wisdom, given me so that I may understand who and what I am in your eternal plan and cycle. I understand that the evolution of our planet is reaching a crisis point, where we will either destroy what we have and return to the primitive state of ten thousand years ago or continue to evolve to be a source of love and substance for our universe as we see it. I present myself in gratitude for the opportunity to be your servant and offer myself as a pathway for your knowledge to reach more and more souls that you lead into my life.

David L. Peters

Continue to open my heart to see those around me who need your love, and give me the courage to be your light to my world as it fits into the most powerful way to bring your presence into our world. I thank you in advance for all that you will do for and with me in the future and the present, one moment at a time, always in the now.

Chapter 3

Our Perceptions Create How We See Our Life

Truly I say to you, whoever says to this
mountain,
"Be taken up and cast into the sea,
And does not doubt in their heart,
But shall believe that what they say
Is going to happen,
It will be granted them."
—Mark 11:23, NASB, neutral gender

I have spoken about abundance and the nature of abundance. Abundance (or not) stems from our basic nature, who we are and the purpose we have in this existence. I have talked about how we are the children of God in the allegoric sense and truly in our very substance. We are a portion of God. Our very being vibrates with the being of God. We are the very image of God, in all that God is.

All that what we call "creation" (and beyond) is spun from the very nature of God. Just like a drop of water in the ocean is part of the ocean, but is not all of the ocean, so we are a part of the being we call God. Like that drop of water, we are not all of God, but we still have the power of God within us. It is a part of us and our very nature. As stated in Genesis, we are the very image of God. That image, being infinite, contains the infinite power that partakes of the essence of what we call God. Indeed, even as the drop of water falling into the ocean creates ripples that extend to the farthest reaches of the ocean, so we, as only drops in the ocean of God, have the capacity to create ripples that extend throughout the reign of God as we can understand it. A mystic is a person who has spent some time living in that oneness of being with God; and as we shall see, we all have had moments or glimpses of that mystical sense during our life.

We will look at this dazzling statement over and over throughout this treatise. It forms the basis of the life of abundance and flies against almost all religions that claim that it is heresy, even though the great mystics of all religions proclaimed it. Even Jesus proclaimed it: *"I have given them the glory that You gave me that they may be one as we are one – I in them and You in me – so that they may be brought to complete unity. Then the world will know that you sent me and have loved them even as you have loved me."* (John 17:22-23,

NIV). The Christian Wisdom teachings operate from this point of truth.

Quite frankly, if the theology we have been taught all of our lives is to hold any truth—that we are sinners shunned by God (even though God still somehow loves us)—then the concept of oneness— all things are one, a portion of the divine, has to be false.

If we are sinners, then we must be separate from God. God apparently has needs that we have failed to meet, causing us to be banished from God's presence. Jesus was so clear in his statements. He understood perfectly well that he and God were one, and he tried many times to tell us that we have this same truth. You are one with God, as I am, in our core.

Jesus claimed that as one *"created in the likeness of God,"* we are one with God—first by proclaiming his oneness with his Father/Mother in heaven and then proclaiming we too have this same power to change reality with just a look. Jesus said, *"If you have faith and do not doubt—you will even say to this mountain, 'Be taken up and cast into the sea,' and it will happen"* (Matt. 21:21, NAB). He also said, *"Whoever believes me will do the works I have been doing, and they will do even greater things than these"* (John 14:12, NIV).

What if Jesus is right? These statements have been proclaimed as just another exaggeration that Jesus was fond of using to get his point across to listeners. That was true when discussing the moral life and the need to forgo the ego, but these statements of oneness were made just before his death when trying to tell his closest friends what to expect in the future. Why would Jesus resort to stretching the possibilities at such a critical time and on such an important matter?

Jesus was saying that we can (and do) control our lives. He said, *"If you have faith and do not doubt."* This key phrase forms the basis of all attempts to live a more conscious life, one that somehow taps into the forces of the universe and guides them to give us our hearts' desire. All attempts—*The Secret,* the laws of attraction, and the various teachings on prosperity—are

> *Believe that life is Worth living, then your Belief will help create The fact.*
> *—William James*

means of bringing wealth and comfort by thinking of it, but they do not bring joy and happiness. But we have the ability to bring ourselves into alignment with the power of the universe and seek what the universe desires to bring to our hearts. Indeed, we can bring joy and happiness into our hearts—regardless of the outward appearances of our lives.

We create our experiences.

We create our existence, our experiences, and our lives. Together we create our world. All we have and do are products of our combined wishes and desires as cognizant beings. Our lives are a product of our individual expectations and desires, and our world conditions are part of our combined expectations and desires as a species. We all know, deep in our hearts, that humanity could erase hunger from our world if we wanted to. We have the food and the means, but we lack the will.

These bold statements stem from our oneness with all that exists. Science has made it clear that all matter is united, exchanging energies, cells, and all parts of life on a daily basis. This makes the entire universe, including you and me, an extended being unto its own.

We have heard often that every cell in our bodies changes, on an average, every seven years or so. I have had a different body (all new cells) ten or twelve times in my lifetime, but I still see myself as myself. I am not different from forty years ago. I'm a little slower perhaps, but otherwise, I am still me. I have a better understanding of the oneness of my self with the self of the universe, but the oneness is there if I see it nor not.

The energies we exude affect everything around us. We are aware of these energies when we have health exams with wires that pick up radiation, heat, and energies that we are always emitting from our bodies. These energies impact the world around us and change the world we live in. We have all experienced the rising temperature in a room when a crowd is present. The energies radiating from our thoughts have an impact on everything around us. This aura forms a pattern around us, and that pattern is a function of our thought patterns that impact all around us, changing as our energies direct.

Our energies effect what occurs in the world—just as science says that the observer of an event affects the outcome of the event. We affect the patterns that emerge in our lives, moment by moment.

What we have and are—our very life conditions—is ours by our very desires, but our unconscious thoughts and desires usually have no direction or goal. Jesus said, *"Greater than this shall you do."* He did not tell us that we need to be alert and awake to be able to direct our patterns in life. We need to trust in our feelings and trust in that power within. The kingdom of God lies within (*the kingdom of God!*)! We can direct that power with confidence that it will be the best it can be.

Trust in God

Abundance comes from trust in the power of God within us. Jesus never doubted that what he proclaimed would occur. Jesus said to the crippled man, *"Take up your bed and go"* (John 5:8, ESV, paraphrased). He had absolute trust (and knowledge) that it would be so. That is the level of trust we need if we are to achieve the results in our lives that Jesus did. *"Greater things than this shall you do"* (John 14:12, NIV, paraphrased). Jesus trusted that it would be so, and his conviction rose out of his very being.

We are sons and daughters of God—portions of God, or as St. Paul put it, we (humanity) are the body of the Christ. We have the fundamental powers of God as part of our very natures (the very image of God, see Genesis 1). It does not require singing, chanting, or repeating slogans to work. It does not require mass acceptance (unless we need this to convince ourselves of our innate power). It does require a level of trust in the goodness of God in our lives to achieve. We will achieve the ultimate results (usually not what we think). The results will be the result we need for our own good and to achieve our underlying beliefs in who we are.

To be in a more powerful place, we need to see what Jesus saw. He did not just trust God to fulfill his requests. He *knew* God would fulfill his requests. What he thought of doing was already done. *"Before you even know it, your Father already knows"* (Matt. 6:8, NIV, paraphrased). His was not hope; it was knowledge that it would be so. When we move to that point, we will be like Jesus. We will be able to tell the mountain to hurl itself into the sea, and it will be so— just as Jesus said it would be.

If we want abundance in our lives, we must change our thoughts about what abundance means. When we are aligned with the universe, we work only to fulfill the purpose of the universe. All else will be granted.

Jesus said, *"Seek first the kingdom of heaven, and all else will be granted you"* (Matt: 6:33, English Revised Version. paraphrased).

To live fully in the kingdom of heaven will be to live into the *"kingdom of God that lies within"* (Luke 17:21, English Revised Version. paraphrased). *"All else will be granted"* (Matt. 6:33, English Revised Version. paraphrased). It won't impress us because that will not be our focus. When we focus on bringing the kingdom of God to be more present in our world, we will be granted sufficient means to do that—one step at a time. At the same time, we will find ourselves happy with our lives, satisfied with what we have, and constantly delighted as more opportunities come into our lives. More creature comforts will be a side benefit.

This is the abundant life.

The kingdom of God lies within.

True abundance comes from within. True abundance fills us with happiness and joy, giving us peace in our minds. It lowers blood pressure, helps us lose weight if we need to, and improves life in every aspect. Life becomes a joy and not a burden. We no longer carry the cross; it becomes a source of resurrection, giving light to the path. We are filled with lightness and joy that cannot be explained. Obstacles become opportunities, and our paths that were rough and twisted become clear and smooth. We only need see the next step in front of us. The things we cringed away from become sources of opportunity and joy.

True abundance does not mean more things and more money. It is the source of intense joy, bliss, and feelings of truth that fill us and inspire us. True abundance is the source of lasting happiness and the joy of knowing that our lives has meaning. We are preparing ourselves for the joy of everlasting bliss. When we dwell in true abundance, we dwell in *"the kingdom that lies within."*

The source of power cannot be denied and will grant us everlasting peace. We find ourselves living in the kingdom of God—paradise on earth.

What more could we want? True abundance is within each of us. No matter our circumstances, we have abundance in our grasp. It is above us, beside us, in front of us, and behind us. It surrounds us. It infuses us as our core energy. It is always within reach if we open our framework of life to see the presence of eternal power.

It is ours for the taking. Do we have the nerve to reach for it? Grasping it requires a shift in existence, thinking, and way of life. Dare we reach to grasp the power that is always there?

Emptiness which is conceptually
Liable to be mistaken for sheer nothingness
Is in fact the reservoir
Of infinite possibilities.
—D.T.Suzuki

Questions to Ponder

How does the proclamation by Jesus that believing we have the power to *"hurl this mountain into the sea"* fit within the framework of your life?

Write down how you could change your perspective on life if you could actually feel that you are safe in the love of God—irrespective of how events are occurring in your life.

Can we see the possibility of changing your perspective to be part of the framework that Jesus spoke about to be *"one without doubt"*?

What do you imagine would happen if you could be without a doubt in the love of God? Do you have the capability to live within the kingdom of God that is within you?

Write down how you would change your life if your faith moved to the point of *"having no doubt."* When you reach that point, material goods will lose their appeal. The kingdom of God will ring true.

Meditation

My Eternal Wisdom, the source of the power that is mine to accept, I am grateful for this opportunity in life to express who I really am. I am life eternal. I am a source and retainer of infinite power. It is mine to grasp and use. I am prostrate in gratitude for this opportunity to express my being in your being, a portion of your everlasting life. I see that, being one with you, I have the ability to fully express who I really am—and use this ability to form my life as I wish. I thank you for this opportunity to express my life in abundance, and I bow in gratitude to be able to consciously form my path for the lifting of all creation. I am grateful for every day that I can experience the love and beauty I see with all my being in this world of physicality.

Chapter 4

A Story of Abundance

***But seek first the kingdom of God and God's
righteousness
And all these things will be added unto you.
—Matthew 6:33, NASB***

I have talked about abundance, but I have not given living examples. In this chapter, I will share some of the times of abundance that have appeared in my life—both before and after my vision in 1967.

God and I had a strong relationship when I was very young, and I recall discussing my life with God when I was four or five years old. We lived in a farming area with no other children my age close by, and I would wander the fields by myself, loving nature, and talking to my invisible friend, God, usually in the form of the young Jesus. I went through a challenge in belief during my early teens, but I came back to belief with a stronger than ever faith by my mid-teens. I continued to talk with God from that point forward, and I still discuss things with God today. God has always responded, but that is another story.

When I was a senior in high school, I was taking college prep courses. I had no idea what I wanted to do with my life. My dad suggested taking a machinist course in the evening, which was being offered at the public high school (I was in a Catholic high school). My father was the foreman of an advanced machine shop. I liked doing things with my hands. I took the course, and I enjoyed it. I had a skill for machines, and when I finished, the instructor asked if I would like an apprenticeship at the small mold-making company where he worked. I accepted, and for the next year, I learned so much. I can still sharpen a drill bit of any size without any guidance but my hands and eyes.

When the Korean War ended, an apprentice who had been drafted into the army came home and wanted his job back. By law, they had to give it to him. The small company had to lay me off. I spend time doing piece machining work when a small machine shop had an order, painting houses and garages, and doing other part-time work.

Dad offered me a job as a testing technician at his place of employment, which made fuel pumps for aircraft. Fall was quickly approaching, and I had no full-time work. I accepted. I found I was a natural at it. In a little over a year, I was the lead technician. I was working on an advanced high-pressure pump with an engineer, designing the test fixture, when he sat me down and insisted that I go to school to be an engineer since I had a gift for this. My parents thought it was a great idea, and so did I. I was twenty-one when I went to college.

College: My Rebranding

This was God working. Losing a job brought me to where I "accidentally" found the skill I was destined for. I had no foresight of this skill, but I thought that being an engineer sounded like interesting work. The biggest change when I went to college was making a "new me." At home and in high school, I was a nerd. I was shy, I stammered, and I was often bullied. I knew I was more than that, and since no one at college knew me, I could be who I wanted to be.

I took a speech course in that first semester, and I learned to accept me for who I was—stammering and all. I still sometimes stammer, but I accept that as part of me, and it does not hinder me from giving talks. I have given hundreds of talks, lectures, and classes. I learned that if I had something to say, it was given to me to say. I often "trod where angels fear to trod."

New Engineer—Synchronicity

I mentioned previously that I had experienced "extraordinary luck" in my first job after college. As Carl Jung would say, I experienced

> *The world is all gates, all opportunities, strings of tension waiting to be struck.*
> *—Ralph Waldo Emerson*

synchronicity, "meaningful coincidences," or "the simultaneous occurrences of events that appear significantly related but have no discernable causal connection."

God continued to work in my life. I followed my instincts for living with expectations and effort. I was always looking ahead and expecting. I never doubted God would give me support. Some people called me lucky, but I knew it was a gift from God, supported by prayers and acceptance. I never felt owed. I accepted and expected that all would be well.

And Still More Synchronicity

I found an apartment in Port Washington, N.Y., on Long Island, and I joined the local church. I discovered the "18–30 Club" for young, single Catholics. Six months later, a beautiful Irish lass walked across the street from her home and joined the club. We were married a little over a year later. It was love at first sight for me—but it took a while to work up the nerve to ask her out. We celebrated our fifty-sixth anniversary this year and raised seven children—to our delight.

God was guiding me to pick that town, find friends, and meet my soul mate.

The Bliss of God

I had a visionary experience in December 1967—just before our fourth daughter was born. I had become a leader in the local chapter of a worldwide movement in the Roman Catholic Church. We had a basic disagreement with the national organization about the direction of the movement. Since it was the New York City and Long Island section, it was a very large and strong group. We had a weekend retreat during the first weekend in December with a group from the national office. I had a long talk with one of the national leaders on Saturday evening. He said, "Are you speaking out of God's will or your own?"

This question was a great dilemma for me. I had always thought I was doing the work of God. Sometime after ten o'clock, I found a tiny chapel with a tabernacle, a single candle, and a small bench. I sat down and asked that question to God—and God answered. I was swept up into a breathtaking embrace of the Cloud of Unknowing for several hours.

When I came out of that at two thirty in the morning, I knew that God would always guide me by putting the teacher before me. Even if the teacher did not know it, I would know. Oh, I had my answer to the question of our group: no change in basic direction since the long view was correct over the immediate problems that beset a large population at that time. We could work on the local level to address the problem without changing the focus of the movement.

And it has always been so.

We were already deeply involved with our faith. The movement aimed at bringing God to everyday life, and that continued. We had a nice house on Long Island, and in the summer of 1970, we decided to take a vacation at a state park in the Finger Lakes Region of New York. We fell in love with the rolling hills, farmland, and beautiful sights. I drove by a big blue building in Binghamton NY and said to my wife, "I would really like to live in this area, but I am a television and visual specialist. Who could use me here?"

That fall, my employer failed to win a contract they were banking on. They had to drastically restructure. They closed the research lab where I worked and laid off 750 engineers from the main operation.

Once again, I was without a job. We had five children to feed. Unlike most others, I accepted what was. I knew I had another job: to find a paying job that could feed and house our family of seven and my wife's mother who lived with us. I knew, deep in my heart, that we were fine. I knew that nothing bad would happen because we had been *"seeking first the kingdom of God,"* and *"all else would be granted"*.

Synchronicity Again

That Sunday, there was a one-inch advertisement in the *New York Times* that had my name all over it. It described my specialized analytic skills to a T. They only ran the ad twice, and I saw it the second time. The address was in Connecticut, but that was all right. I answered. A few weeks later, I was asked for an interview. It was in upstate Binghamton, New York; the Connecticut address was for the headhunter who ran the ad. At the interview I recognized the building we had passed when I expressed my wishes to live there, and that building was the location of my potential employer. I was hired, and we moved to our present location in 1971.

God really does respond to a person's desires, if properly put, without demands—but with expectations. We had wanted to raise our children in a more natural setting than Long Island. We wanted to be able to give our children a ready source for the joy of nature. God adjusted our lives to permit that to occur. I was laid off, but God used that period to move us where God had led us the preceding summer. *"Before you ask, I shall answer"* (Isaiah 65:24).

We made no demands of any type on place or anything else. We expected that we would find a good place where we could continue to follow God's will as we understood it—and raise our family in a good atmosphere.

These are only examples of things God has given us. *"Search first for the kingdom of God, and all these things will be granted you."*

I am no master. I am a long way from that, but I have taken several steps, small as they are, toward that goal. I am an Enneagram 8, which tends to dominate and bulldoze all opposition. I often have to apologize for injuring relationships.

God knows I am trying—even when my mouth is running off with itself, carrying me along with it.

> ***Life isn't about finding yourself.***
> ***Life is about creating yourself.***
> ***—George Bernard Shaw***

Questions to Ponder

Have you had moments when things seemed to happen that were just right? Those are times of synchronicity. Write down the times you can recall.

Have some of these moments caused a shift that would not have occurred if these odd occurrences had not happened?

Have you thought that the occurrences were given to you by the driving force of the universe? Can we call it God?

Write down how that thought feels to you in the deepest part of your being.

Meditation

Thank you, God, for your continued gifts of life that you have showered upon me. I bow my head and body in gratitude for life, all of life, even when there appeared to be no way out of a bad situation. You continued to surprise me with joy and life—and then more joy and life. I accept the limitations that have crept upon me and realize they are a part of the pattern of life. I give thanks for all you have showered upon me during this cycle of life. I rejoice to be part of the evolution of life in my universe. I can see and experience the unfolding of life, eventually reaching its fullness of being. The cycle of humanity continues. I only need to open my heart and mind and soul to reach the ultimate knowledge of my oneness with you, our Eternal Wisdom.

I bow my head in gratitude for my life. You have showered me with love and grace, surprising me at every turn. I understand now that everything has been in perfect harmony for what I came to do and how I came to grow, and I am awed by the perfection.

Chapter 5

Trust in the Goodness of God

*Whoever takes the lowly position of this child
is the greatest in the kingdom of heaven.
—Matthew 18:4, NIV*

*T*he challenge is to learn to trust and find the way to *"the kingdom of God that lies within."* Are there processes or techniques that ease us into that level, smooth the way, and create opportunities to find that level of trust?

Jesus said, *"You must become like a child"* (Matt. 18:3, NIV, paraphrased). He is talking about a child's level of trust. The kind of trust that says, "God, the Eternal Wisdom, can do no wrong, will let no wrong be done to me (my soul), and desires only love and joy for me." A child, if given half a chance in life, looks at his or her parents in this light. The child believes that the parents can do no wrong, will let no wrong be done to them, and desire only love and joy for them. If we look into the eyes of a child, we see love and trust shining forth in abundance. They expect only to be loved and treated tenderly.

All seven of our children loved to be picked up and swung or tossed into the air and caught, squealing with delight and laughter. They knew I would not drop them and would protect them from harm. They knew I loved them with all my being. One of my greatest joys was when we had four little girls at home—with only five years separating the oldest from the youngest. I'd come home from work and be surrounded by laughing bundles of joy. They all wanted to be picked up, hugged, swung, and loved.

Trust as only a child trusts.

Jesus said, *"Become like a child."* Trust in the love of God. God spun the universe out of the very being of God, the same God who spun us out of the very fabric of God. We carry within us the genes of God. Our DNA is the DNA of God. We are *"made in the image and likeness of God"* (Genesis 1:27, NIV, gender-neutral). Who else can we trust?

People say, *"Let go and let God."* It is so true, but few really believe it is true. We say the words, but we only live the words in desperation. It requires full abandonment of our egos and all that we now think of ourselves as being worthy and competent, or, too often, unworthy and incompetent. Deep in our hearts, we suspect we are anything but worthy and competent. We have been told over and over that we are not worthy at the core of our being. By throwing out the junk we feed ourselves when we say that we are not worthy—and throwing ourselves into the effort— we will find that we *are* worthy and competent on a level we did not realize we had.

"I am made in the image and likeness of the Divine Creator." I recently experienced that effect. I had been given a serious task. To save one my closest friends, I had to tear him down to face reality before he could begin to heal. My friend had a serious problem and could not face it or seek proper help. I sought aid to help, and was told that I was the only person in a position to help; therefore, it was mine to intercede. I beseeched God for help and trusted God would respond as God has always done in the past.

I still had much angst on the last evening before I planned to approach my friend. I was not sure I could do it. I was not sure if I had the right words. Almost all people have doubts in serious situations, especially if one has never done an intervention before. The evening before I planned the event, my wife and I went to a talk. The person said wonderful things about trying to change the world—one step at a time. The talk lasted ninety minutes, and a few words changed everything for me. She said, *"If you are a true friend to someone who is destroying themselves and they do not understand that, then you must tell them, despite the pain. For that is what a true friend is: you are their friend, through thick and thin, and this is the thin."*

God was speaking to me. God will speak to me in my most desperate times—if I listen. Her words were just a tiny fraction of the talk. God was assuring me that it was time. I would be guided if I trusted.

The next morning, I was still not sure when or how I could do it. I was totally at peace. It would happen, but the timing was out of my hands. My friend spoke a few words to me that rang a bell. It felt like God picked me up and picked up the notes I had so carefully worked on. He led us to a room where I could close the door and talk. God flowed through me into the other. We ended up hugging and crying. I was thanked wholeheartedly, and we separated.

The process of intervention does not end with the first talk. It does not end at the second talk. If we call ourselves a friend, then we will be that friend when the ice is thin. My presence in the life of my friend was a task given by our Creator, and I acted accordingly. I trust God will continue to work out for the best for us all, especially for my friend. I will be part of the process for the rest of our lives.

God is speaking all time, but who listens?

That is how trust works. If we listen, we will be guided. It all is working perfectly. If we have a role in something, we will be shown the opportunity to be there and do what we are meant to do. This does not mean that we do nothing. We work with what we see at all times. If something calls us, we must respond. If someone interjects with information, we act. I spent two days writing my notes and getting reactions from my wife and others who knew the situation. When the time came, I knew exactly what I was going to say. I could give the person my notes and examples of the behavior in question to study after I had spoken.

I trusted God. That was all I had left. I had done everything I could do.

That is how it works. We do all we can, and God will do the rest, including guiding me in any steps to aid my friend. This is serious, and it could have very serious results in my friend's life. That is something else that will be helped over time. The friend is my friend, now and forever, and I will not let it go of my friend. It is in God's hands, and the best result will happen for us both.

> *I know God will not give me anything I can't handle. I just wish that God didn't trust me so much.*
> *—Mother Teresa*

This is abundance for my friend and for me. By facing the truth of the life my friend was living, he could have a chance to find internal peace and face life again—one day at a time. I know it will happen in the future. I trust that God will lead the way. That is what trust is. I trust when the outcome is in doubt, but the outcome will be the right one for all. We are trying to grow in God and wisdom.

Nothing is by chance.

The Divine Spirit places us in situations where, if we are alert, we will see how our gifts of friendship will be of service. If we trust in God, knowing that nothing is left to chance, we will see opportunities to be of God's service as they arise.

I have missed many opportunities, and I have often been given the chance to see how I could have played a more important part in some actions. These missed opportunities provide guidance to me in the future. I miss more opportunities than I accept, but I also recognize that these opportunities will continue to rise before me until I rejoin God.

Trust in the Divine Spirit is the most important key in finding abundance. Peace and joy come with an awareness of the closeness of the Eternal Spirit with our physical lives. There is no separation. God and I are one. God and you are one. Therefore, you and I are one. You and I are made in the image of God—and so are the seven billion other souls on our planet and the potentially hundreds of billions of souls in the universe.

> *To live is the rarest thing in the world.*
> *Most people exist, that is all.*
> *—Oscar Wilde*

Questions to Ponder

Try to think about how trust in Divine Wisdom guides your life.

Write down the areas where you are afraid to trust to your wisdom.

Imagine how your life would shift if you could trust that Divine Wisdom will always lead you to the right solution.

Write down how your life would change if you had total trust in Divine Wisdom to guide you.

Pick one or two areas of your life you could put into the hands of Divine Wisdom.

Write down the areas of your life that you are going to place in the hands of Divine Wisdom.

Return to these areas once a day for the next thirty days—and keep track of how these areas of your journey are behaving.

Meditation

My Eternal Wisdom, I bow in gratitude for the guidance you gave me in the past. I bow in gratitude for this wonderful abundance—if we see that gift of abundance in all the glory that it is, no matter what it seems at the first glance. Thank you, God, for giving me the gift of speech, for guiding my words and tongue. This is all I could ask—nothing more than to be the vehicle of your love to my friend in this time of need. You have shown me the true meaning of abundance, not just more things but more Spirit. I have the capacity to do your will and be your vehicle for the truth. We can all find peace and joy in your presence.

I am in gratitude that I have the needs of our earth brought before me to examine and act where I can. I know that you will show me how I can serve you and Mother Earth. The increasing pain of Mother Earth is portrayed by the instant communication available today. If I listen to you in my heart, I will see the blessings that await me.

I have watched how the gift of trust in your blessings has blessed my life—even when it is hard to see. I have learned this lesson by all the blessings I have seen if I just accept what has occurred as a blessing rather than the terror it first seemed. I thank you for the gift of acceptance and the sense of peace that accompanies that gift. I ask that everyone see this blessed peace. It releases all the stress that destroys our lives.

Thank you.

Chapter 6

Trust Is No Accident

Continuous efforts—
not strength or intelligence—
is the key to unlocking our potential.
—Winston Churchill

*H*ow do we put ourselves in a place where abundance is present in our lives? Well, there are many ways, but I can only talk of the path I have followed for most of my life. This is the path that led me to abundance, joy and happiness, and led me to understand what abundance is.

It requires practice to walk a path where I am filled with bliss for no outward reason. The light seems brighter, things seem to happen like miracles every day, and joy fills my being much of the time. It requires time and skills. It requires willingness and the desire to walk this path.

The path is time and intention.

I have tried to spend about an hour a day, every day, on some type of spiritual presence for almost fifty years. I have learned that there are many ways to turn our attention outside of ourselves. It can be in meditation, reading, exercise, driving, listening to enriching music, walking, laughing, or even praying!

What makes an event spiritual? It all lies in the *intention* that we have going into that event. Without that intention, no matter how the event appears on the outside, it is a waste of time. Appearing to be in prayer for the purpose of appearing to be in prayer is a negative. Intention is the key for something to be spiritual. A spiritual event is spiritual because a person intends it to be spiritual. The person has an intention to bring God to that event consciously so that joy and love are there. God is rarely mentioned in most of these events, but the essence of God—love—is present and flowing over all. Reading these thoughts can be a spiritual experience if that is your intention.

I was not always in a spiritual mood or a God-centered thinking process, but I would read and pray for an hour each day, with the intention that, no matter how I felt, this was a moment I would place myself, somehow, into the presence of my God. I would read, pray, and read some more. I would walk out to my car with my lunch, read, and think about what I read. If I could not think, I would reread what I had before me. I spent the time—no matter how bland it seemed. The act suffices for intention; committing to prayer time ensures that intention is operating.

Just do it!

Those hours literally saved my life. I would spend periods in depression, without knowing that it was depression. When those moments of depression went away, I was a notch higher than before the episode. I was feeling the presence. I was eager to continue the process. I was able to read books and understand them at new levels. I was able to hear others and understand the pain and joy they were feeling.

The low periods usually did not last long, but once they lasted for several years. I persevered in my hourly process during that time, and I learned that God is always there—whether we can feel God's presence or not. I trusted in the love of God. Eventually, the process won. God is present all the time—day or night. When I wake up in the middle of the night (and one of joys of aging is the frequency of waking during the night increases), I always feel the presence of God within and around me.

I did not have to wait fifty years for God to bring me abundance. God was filling my life with abundance from a very young age—more than seventy-nine years that I can remember. God is always willing to give and is waiting to be asked by our souls. God is always filling our lives with our deepest desires, usually unknown to ourselves. The universe is always responding to our quests—no matter how things seem. We must let that quest from our souls become more conscious, and our openness to God will be central in our lives.

Seek first the kingdom.

Abundance is always internal. *"Seek first the kingdom of God, and all else will be given to you."* (Matt. 6:33, NASB). These words define abundance in its essence. The hour a day shaped my feelings and knowledge of abundance. I did not ask God for money or anything in particular. I asked for the ability to be the presence of God to others. Intention sets the framework for all to bring the joy of God into our lives, and intention lets God work through our very beings.

Abundance stems from the internal. Jesus said, *"Seek first the kingdom of God: then all else will be given you."* He also said, *"The kingdom of God is within."* What is more abundant than the kingdom of God? Abundance is within. If we feel filled with abundant love of God, then we are overflowing with abundance. When we feel filled with abundance, everything we need will be granted us—without asking, seeking, or desiring.

Don't get me wrong. I am no master. I still desire a comfortable life. I still like nice things. Much to my surprise, I have more nice things

I just kept on doing what everyone else starts out doing. The question is, why did the other people stop?
—William Stafford

than I ever thought I would have. I am constantly amazed by how comfortable we are in life at this stage. We are surrounded by beauty. We both have fairly good health, and we have a strong zest for life. I see that abundance is part of the basic fruits of life. *"Seeking the kingdom of God"* has been a center of our lives for over fifty years. And we have found *"all else has been given to us."*

Finding the Kingdom within

So, how does one start? Do you have to wait fifty years to see results? No! Start *"seeking the kingdom of God"* today, and God will respond today. Do not stop seeking. The response will not occur unless the quest for the kingdom is ongoing. Spend time setting intention. Spend time filling your mind and heart with blessed words. Spend time in silence, listening for the whisper of God. Do it every day—even when there seems to be no response.

There are many books that can fill your being with light. Even fifteen minutes of reading each day brings light into the darkness. It lets the shadow be free and calms the demons that exist in each of us. Take a walk in the woods or around the block. Play with children to see God shining forth. There are an infinite number of ways to place yourself in the presence of God. Just do it.

God will bring you abundance until you pass into the exciting realm of the absolute—and then you get to do it all over again.

> ***Never be afraid to trust***
> ***An unknown future to a known God.***
> **—Corrie ten Boom**

Questions to Ponder

Have you found yourself starting something that seemed exciting for a while and then seemed boring— even though you knew it was good that you did it?

What was your reaction? Did you continue even though it seemed boring? Did you try to find a new way to make it fresh or did you abandon the effort? Write it down. If you could have found a new way but didn't, why not?

Does the idea of finding *"the kingdom within"* seem exciting? Do you sense the presence of God in your soul? Write down how that potential feels inside your being.

Meditation

Thank you, my Eternal Wisdom. You bring me peace and joy in life. You have shown me that life is eternal, death is but a passage into the next step of living, and all I wish is part of my very being if I but look inward.

Thank you for showing me the kingdom within. It is mine for the asking. You open my eyes to the truth. You give me the light that reveals my shadows and brings them into the light so I can live in the light of abundance. Thank you for showering me with abundance.

Chapter 7

Ego Abundance

For I say to you if you have the faith of a
mustard seed,
you will say to this mountain "Move from
here to there,"
and it will move, and nothing will be
impossible to you.
—Matthew 17:20, ESV

I have been talking about abundance from a different point of view from what is most popular. Two forms of abundance work in different styles with differing results. The first is ego abundance, and the second is soul abundance.

Ego Abundance

Ego abundance or ego-based abundance is a popular method of attempting to use the creative power of our being to bring us things that we believe will make us happy. We believe money, power, a specific potential lover, or other specific goal will bring us happiness. The power of positive thinking is sometimes called the law of attraction, the abundance prayer, or the prosperity gospel. They feed the desires of the ego to generate personal desires, wealth, power, and control.

A way to recognize ego abundance (or ego-based abundance) is the use of a key phrase similar to "attract all you desire by following these steps." Note the word *desire*. That is the ego speaking—not the soul. All such ego-based programs are based upon desires, and desires are often personal ego trips, usually for money or power, or demanding that a specific someone be attracted to us.

These approaches work when pursued as a goal for a personal purpose. The power of positive thinking has been used since Norman Vincent Peale's book on the subject. There are large groups in and out of various religions that stress the power of positive thinking and eliminating negative thought patterns that can govern our lives, reduce stress, and give us a fresh view of the world.

But much of the hoopla surrounding these teachings depends on convincing the follower to follow a brainwashing approach of creating lists and/or goals, setting power goals, and using chanting, dancing, or mantras to suppress negativity. Now I believe strongly in the use of mantras, but not for the purpose of creating personal wealth, etc.

These practices can be useful. Do they work? Sometimes they do. They always work for leaders who become prosperous and lack for nothing. These enchanters line their own pockets.

We create our own lives. We are driving our own buses, and they sometimes appear to work. Money comes, jobs appear, and other testimonies can be gathered. Many of the mega-churches that preach the prosperity line contain well-off, fairly young people who respond enthusiastically to these events. They drive nice cars, have well-paying jobs, and live dynamic lives. And if someone fails, loses a job, or has a serious illness, it is the person's fault for not having sufficient faith in the teachings of the leader. Give more money and change your negative attitude—and all will be well—despite the reality of the present condition.

More, More

These events, churches, and groups seem to work because they are using (or misusing) the power of abundance. Abundance is always there. If we believe it in our inner being, it will be done. Jesus said, *"Truly I say to you, whoever says to this mountain, 'Be taken up and cast into the sea,' and shall not doubt in their heart, but believes that what they say will take place, it will be done."* That is true—no matter how that faith is couched.

Faith must come from the deepest part of our lives, and it is possible to misuse that faith for personal gain. If we work hard enough, we can convince ourselves that we deserve these things, and they will make us happy if we achieve them.

And they do make us happy.

For a while.

Then they do not.

Then we want more. More of the same, or something else.

Then we will be happy.

Until we are not.

Then we cycle again.

Without the assistance of the Divine Being... I cannot succeed, with that assistance, I cannot fail.
—Abraham Lincoln

Ego abundance does not provide lasting joy.

We can convince ourselves that these things are all we need to be happy. Large crowds, intense music, hard-driving speeches, promises, chanting, and self-hypnosis are used to bring the emotions to a peak and suppress the analytic portion of our minds, usually so we will come back for another charge the next night or the next week.

These emotions can tap into the infinite energy stream that flows in and around us to create the very things we think we crave. And they will be created. But the things we so desperately thought would bring us joy and happiness eventually pale. They only bring us boredom, exhaustion, discontent, and sadness.

We try again because we know "this" will be the answer that will bring joy, internal peace, and an everlasting sense of accomplishment. When that fails, we go on to the next thing.

If not this, then that.

Eventually we are worn out, all of our adrenaline has been spent, and the rallies fail to move us. Some can go on for many years at that level, but most tire of them in a few years or months. They drift off in a daze and try to find something else to generate the energy level they need to feed upon.

And they will find it in the next speaker, the next church, or the next promise of money, power, and happiness.

If we look carefully at this process, it looks suspiciously like an addiction: a high, a period where we return to normal, and then another high. Instead of a chemical, it is a method to raise our adrenaline levels. We must have that shot again and again—until we burn out and the shot fails to have any effect. I have seen this with speaking in tongues and dancing around in mega-churches. They have massive singing and dancing groups that gather for the purpose of achieving personal goals, usually prosperity or 'abundance'.

I enjoy them as much as anyone. One of my favorite methods of prayer or being with God is with music.

A good song gives me a good jolt and a high. I love energetic music and a rousing sermon or talk at a service. I love the energy and spirit of a gathering, the life of the Holy Spirit that exudes at a good gathering, and the occasional convention where thousands are caught up in the Holy Spirit.

I do not need it every day. Those events do not feed the day-to-day force of life. They are like a trip to the ice cream shop. Those high-spirited events feed the soul and bring excitement to the spirit.

Finding Soul Food

I also love the sung mantras. I find great meaning in the older Sanskrit approach that I have found in Deva Premal and Miten music and meditations. Gentle flowing music can work wonders and soothe the soul. I listen to them every day I can. I also listen to Deepak Chopra's meditations as often as I can. But these experiences only form a part of program that brings us lasting joy and happiness.

These high experiences are not the basic elements that bring us lasting peace and joy. These emotional highs become the focus of the user of ego abundance. They form the crux of life to achieve a goal that has been set in the ego. People following this pattern almost always eventually become exhausted and are unable to continue. They remember the exciting interlude that met their expectations at that moment, but it is a bit disappointing in the conclusion. They go back whence they came, sometimes to try again, but too often to become absorbed by the events of day-to-day life. They become lost in the perceived trials of living.

**The Ego is a veil
Between humans and God.
—Rumi**

Questions to Ponder

How do we feel about the concept of abundance? Are we disappointed when we hear that true abundance does not necessarily mean wealth and worldly goods?

Write down your feelings on this topic.

Do you recognize your ego-driven needs that have little to do with true happiness?

Write down what you believe could give you joy in life.

Examine your entry to see if it is driven by ego.

Meditations

My Eternal Spirit, you have shown me the path of perseverance and inwardness. You have shown me the errors of the ego, especially as espoused in the ego-abundance approach to an abundant life. I am grateful for not having fallen into these enticing paths, but you have led me to see your face everywhere, your being in all things. Your presence is always before me, in me, behind me, around me, and filling me—if I am aware of that presence or not. I am so grateful for the moments where I have been aware of your presence and feeling your wonder and love move within me. You give me peace and joy no matter what is going in my life. Your presence in all of the cosmos and in everything around me has kept me grounded in your love all these years. I am in wonder at seeing your love manifest itself in my life, and I am looking forward to all that happens.

Chapter 8

Soul Abundance

In God I trust; I shall not be afraid.
—Psalm 56, ESV

S oul abundance rises from the soul. Jesus said, "Seek first the kingdom of God, and all else will be given to you" (Matt. 6:33, ESV).

Soul abundance rises spontaneously from seeking first the kingdom of God. Soul abundance rises from our inner eyes turned to see God in all things and seeing the good in all things. Soul abundance fills us with joy and wonder. It gives us the capacity to cast our worries aside. No matter what it seems like in the middle of the event, we will rise to the next level of living—even if the next level means passing from the physical realm. Death is a good thing; it frees our souls from the vibrational constraints of physical life and four dimensions. It allows us to experience the boundless freedom of the ultimate realm of God.

Trust in God

When we practice soul abundance, we do not have to make lists or determine what things and how much we need to be happy. God understands what gives us happiness, eases the load, brings us joy, and fills the void we all carry inside. We fill that void with love—spilling out and overflowing into life. God understands what "All else" we need to gain the abundant life.

I understand that we need things at times. I have learned to trust and believe God will supply these things when we need them if we do our part to open the way for fulfillment. I remember back when we had an unexpected bill for a furnace repair. We were putting three kids through college, and we did not have a thousand dollars. We trusted (and expected) that God would find a way to solve the situation in the best way for all concerned. We went away on Saturday, and when returned that evening, we had a message from a charity we had recently bought some raffle tickets from. We had won the grand prize of, yes, a thousand dollars. Lucky? No. God gave us something in return for our trust and expectation. I had bought hundreds of raffle tickets through the years, and I had never won any prize—let alone a grand prize.

That is how soul abundance works. It does not require lists, drilling repetitive phrases to eliminate doubt, high-adrenaline shocks, and mental gymnastics to keep concentrating on our desires. All it requires is doing what we can do, giving the problem over to the

Divine Wisdom, and letting it go. We know that the best possible result will occur. Let it go—and trust. The best will occur if we trust and let our hearts be wrapped in the cushion of God's love.

Surprise, Surprise

The best is often not what we expect. Many times, it turns out to have a twist that seems doubtful at the time, but it turns out for the best that could be—usually far better than if the original desire had taken place. My partner and I own a small high-technology company, building a computer graphics engine to train pilots. It is a very high-end program, and we depend heavily on government purchases. When the government shut down in October 2013, all contracts stopped for almost one year. To put it mildly, that put a strain on our resources. We had received help from our bank off and on previously, but when we went to them that time, we were refused. They felt it was too risky, not knowing when the contracts were coming again. We were concerned since we had done all we could. Our salesperson was one of the best in the industry, but so little was occurring in the industry. Two of our competitors had gone under. I turned it over to the Divine Wisdom; we had twenty employees who could lose jobs and twenty families who would be without paychecks. Within a week after the bank said no, we received a call from our biggest customer. They wanted to put us on their "favored" list and would buy a significant amount from us to cement the deal. We had a major payment due on a Monday, and the money arrived in our checking account on the preceding Thursday so we could pay the bill on Friday.

We had the money and did not go into debt. What seemed like a blow when the bank said no turned out for the best. We are flourishing with our bottom line.

God helps businesses pay their employees. God looks into our hearts and sees what is present. Are we concerned only for ourselves? Do our wishes and desires have to do with the best for others? Eternal Wisdom understood our love and

> *I will not fear, for you are ever with me, and you will never leave me to face my perils alone.*
> *—Thomas Merton*

concern for others, stepped in before we asked, and made something wonderful happen. My partner and I also benefited, but that was not our main concern. Part of my search for "the kingdom of God" includes other families that depend on continued employment.

"For do not worry about tomorrow, for tomorrow will take care of itself. Each day has its own problems" (Matt 6:34, ESV, paraphrased).

Take one step at a time.

I have been asked often if I worry. Sometimes—before an answer appears—I can lose sight of what I know is true. I start to worry and be concerned. That is when I turn to my spiritual sources, reading and meditation, and sink into their warmth and comfort. I sometimes wake up at three in the morning and fret. I sink into a walking meditation until I arrive at the point where I know that all will be good and well—no matter what happens. One of my sons noticed that I was just so accepting of what was happening. I would move to the next step and then the next step without worrying.

We create context from our inner resources. *"As you believe, you will receive"* (Matt. 21:22, NIV, paraphrased). That is how it is, and we set our own contexts to live and create our own lives. I know that God will always be with me, and he will lead me through this life into the next experience, a rebirth into eternity and beyond.

Soul abundance rises from our very essence, and meshes with life and all that exists to produce the very best for us. Yes, it does require trust! Part of the reason I have that level of trust is that I have seen it work so many times in the past. I have referenced some of these in previous chapters, but my whole life has been filled with them—from small things to amazing big things. We have to spend the time to develop that trust and reliance, but it is not difficult. It becomes a joyful process of living in the presence of God. Spending time with God becomes a joy and brings us to comfort and peace.

> *Have enough courage to trust love*
> *One more time and always*
> *One more time.*
> *—Maya Angelou*

Questions to Ponder

Jesus said, *"Do not worry about tomorrow."* Does this seem possible?

Write down how you feel about that.

Write down how your life could shift if you did not worry about tomorrow.

Meditation

My Eternal Wisdom, you have filled me today with peace and joy beyond compare. I do not worry about how much longer I will be in this physical body. I have eternity to dwell in your love and bliss. I have so much gratitude for the privilege of being shown the possibility of your love and joy for so many years. I yearn to share the vision with others so they can see the joy in life that is possible. I ask your blessing on this path. I want to share your yearning for all humanity and remove the veil that blinds us to your love.

Chapter 9

Living Abundantly

Seek first the kingdom of God, and all these
things will be given to you.
Do not worry about tomorrow.
Each day has sufficient troubles of its own.
—Matthew 6:33-34, NASB

I have been talking about abundance as if it is a reality, but I have not spent sufficient time explaining what abundance is—or even if it exists in any form. Jesus said, *"All these things will be given to you."* How can that be? We see so much trouble around us, and we may be experiencing trouble as we read this. What is behind this strange phrase? Jesus died a painful death while *"seeking the kingdom of God."*

Was Jesus seeking the kingdom of God at the time of his death? Maybe he was living in that kingdom of God despite what was happening before our eyes. A feeling of abundance is an internal sense that all is going well and that all will be well, no matter the external appearance. A sense of lacking is an internal sense of not enough.

Perception

Two people can view the same event differently. The loss of a job can seem devastating during the event, but it can be seen as a blessing when new opportunities open up. One can hunker down, retreat, and wait out the loss before starting over. The loss of a job can feel so devastating that one gives up and retreats from life, thinking it is not worth the effort.

Acceptance

Jesus was talking about perception, trust, and knowing. If I trust that God will not desert me and let me down, God will lead me to other events that will be blessings. I will be filled with abundance, peace, and joy. This sequence has never failed me, and it will

> *Everything has its wonders, even darkness and silence, and I learn, whatever state I may be in, therein to be content.*
> *—Helen Keller*

not fail you. It requires acceptance of the event! This event occurred, and it is good—despite how it may appear—and it is simply an event in the flow of life. This event will lead to another event, and that too will be good, no matter what it appears to be at the moment.

What should our reaction be? Thank God for this blessing for it is a blessing in disguise. Even what we call death is a blessing.

Expectation

After acceptance comes expectation of the best. I know that the end result will be the best possible outcome for my journey. Nothing could be better for what I am trying to accomplish in my journey.

It all starts with perception. We must perceive that God wishes only good for us. God never sends us a trial to test us. God gives us all the means to accomplish our inner goals. These events lead us to the results we need to climb to the next level.

How does this happen? What we wish for in the core of our being is what occurs in our lives.

We are the creators of our lives.

We create our lives. If we perceive an event as being perfect, we will leave that event with a positive approach that will lead to more perfect events.

It all lies in perception. As we perceive, so it is! It is that simple. Jesus said, *"If you have the faith of a mustard seed, and say to that mountain, hurl yourself into the sea, it will occur."*

Jesus also said, *"Greater things than this shall you do."*

Jesus understood that all we perceive we put there ourselves. It can be a combined process, but we are ultimately responsible for our lives. We determine what our lives consist of.

Our lives are what we make them. God places choices before us all the time. The choices we make determine the path of our life. Genesis 1 states that we are the image of God. And one of God's most prominent forces is that God is the Creator, causing all of what we call reality to spin out of nothing. As an image of God, we are creators too! Deep in our souls, we desired the events that we are living in right now. These desires stem from our very being, and they are derived from choices we made in the past.

How can we desire our lives? This seems impossible, but the universe is constructed to give us our very desires—no matter how strange. If we deeply believe we don't deserve to have something, we probably won't have it. The universe follows our desires, and we often desire things or events that prove negative to our true needs. We think we need more of this or that to be happy—wealth, cars, a bigger house—but these things will not make us happier for long. We can work to bring these things to us, but the joy we achieve doesn't last. We seek more wealth, bigger cars, and bigger houses, and the result is a deep feeling of lack, of something missing.

Albert Einstein said, *"We cannot solve our problems with the same thinking that created them."* If we want to achieve lasting peace and joy, find the kingdom of God, and have true abundance, we change our thoughts from what led us to where we are to thinking about where we want to be.

We achieve our deepest desires.

We achieve what we want. Even our passing is part of that thinking. Our souls know when we have achieved what we came here to do and makes the decision for us. We put ourselves in the position to leave this world and move to the spirit world.

The universe is eager to do our bidding. We are *"made in the image and likeness of God."* God is the Creator. If God is love, then love is the Creator of all there is. God is willing to give itself to all there is. If God is the Creator, and we are made in the *"image and likeness of God,"* what else is there for us to be but a Creator? And what do we create but our lives, in love? Who else creates our lives? Why would God create for us when Cod made us in the image and likeness of the great Creator? What is our purpose but to create?

And so it is.

All we are and all we do is part of the creation process. Nothing that is not of our creation exists. And that applies to all seven billion of us. All seven billion people self-create their individual lives, each choosing a path for what we came to accomplish on this path of physicality. Our paths mix at our own choosing. Nothing is by chance. All of creation is a mix. Our creations provide the path for the next step in this wondrous universe.

We create our lives and our patterns of living. This marvelous pattern of life is the essence of our being. And we control it—consciously or unconsciously. It is our choice.

For after all, the best thing one can do
Whenever it is raining is to let it rain.
—Henry Wadsworth Longfellow

Questions to Ponder

Imagine if you could nudge your life in a new direction.

Write down how you imagine your life changing if things started improving.

"Seek first the kingdom of God." What does this mean to you?

Write down how this could change your life.

How would total acceptance of your life as it is right now change your perception of your life?

Meditation

My Divine Creator, I bow in gratitude for the beneficence of your creation in my life. I, who feel my way almost blindly in my passing through time, cannot see the future, but I see the past and the wonderful now. I see the events that have brought me here, and I trust, and yes I know, that the path in the future will bless and fill my heart with joy and peace. Give me the acceptance and certainty that will keep my will firmly in the path of internal joy and love. For this I thank and bless you.

Yes, it is so.

Chapter 10

The Nature of Abundance

So God created humanity in God's own image;
In the image of God, God created them.
Male and female God created them.
—Genesis 1:27, NIV, gender neutral

The concept of abundance seems counterintuitive to the linear nature of thinking that is taught by our standard education system. We are taught to look at first causes and extract concepts from each progressive step in nature and determine the following step. We are limited to prevent us from thinking too far ahead. God forbid that a genius appears since that person sees far beyond what is pedantically presented in school. The genius sees what could be, seeing the twist of nature that permits the next giant leap in thought. The type of thinking is deeply frowned upon in most schools.

Steve Jobs did not do well in school. He was a true genius and quickly summed up what was being presented and leaped into the future. His adoptive parents permitted him to progress at his own pace and do what he needed to do to further his driven personality. That genius gave us the graphic interface, fonts as a graphic tool, an affordable mouse, and a low-cost interface mechanism in the first Mac. If you have never seen the original TV ads for the Mac in the 1984 Super Bowl, you should search for it and see it. It is a great example of presenting the future in a mind-blowing fashion. That Mac changed all personal computers forever, and we cannot conceive of a different approach and look.

Steve Jobs changed so much of modern life: the iPod, the iPhone, the iPad, and a whole new way of working. He raced after multiple dreams, ignoring all the naysayers and achieving success.

The Image of God

Abundance works in a nonlinear fashion. Abundance stems from our basic nature and not from the process of thinking in a linear fashion. God is the resident genius that each of us contains—no matter what our education or IQ—and is that part of the essence that makes us human and conscious.

God, the Divine Wisdom, created humanity in a divine fashion. *"God created humanity in the image of God; in the Divine Image God created humanity, male and female God created them"* (Genesis 1:27, NIV, gender neutral). I repeat this quote often because it forms the fundamental thought of abundance. It is similar to all major religions in presenting humanity as an extension of God in some form, but most religions shy from extending that to the level I state here.

We are created in the image of God! What stronger language can be used? Oh yes, Jesus said, *"Greater things than this you shall do"* (John 14:12, NIV).

We are creators.

What is the fundamental nature of God? God is the Creator! Out of Love, God creates. What does that make our fundamental nature? We are the creators of all that we are. We are the creators of our lives.

This concept certainly flies against all we have been taught and all we perceive. Out first thought is: "This cannot be so, for we would not have created our present lives if we were doing the creation." So many things seem wrong when we look upon our lives.

How can we be the creators of our lives? Did we create our secrets and the shadows that haunt us day and night? I created these monsters? I created the life I live? I created the obstacles of my life? I created these physical and mental pains? I created these moods, daydreams, and the reality of my day-to-day existence?

I created every one of them. I also created all the joys I see, the songs I love, and the love I share. I created everything—both good and bad—in my life. Perhaps in joining with the creative powers of others; but without my creative input, I would never have seen all that is around me.

The kingdom of God creates.

"The kingdom of God lies within" (Luke 17:21, KJV). The kingdom of God is the state of God's behavior, our ability to think and reason, the reason we see beauty and love. We create constantly, through the perception of our lives. There is no other thing but the life we create. We always create the life we need right now. Everything is always perfect in that sense, but our perceptions lead to the next perception, which is based upon the previous perception—unless we decide to shift that next perception into a new direction.

The choice is ours.

We have a choice. It is ours to take in each moment. We have the choice to move up, down, left right, forward, or backward. We can take a leap, jump into the unknown, and lean on God to make that choice.

We have a choice in every moment. We can

> **Without risk, faith is an impossibility.**
> **—Soren Kierkegaard**

choose to stay where we have been, where it feels comfortable, or we can choose to squint, see the possibility, and leap into the unknown. How often have we leaped into the unknown? Do we dare? Have we dared to venture and tried to see? It does not always work out like we hoped, but the experience is always worth the chance.

I have taken a risk many times in my life. Once I joined forces with my beloved, we agreed to mutually risk for opportunities.

Twice we have started a high-technology business with others. Once the risk was overtaken by another technology that caused us to fail in 1969, but the knowledge gained was stored away. When we tried again in 1996, it has worked well.

This willingness to risk allows us to risk trusting God to help us through difficult times. We have risked much when we stepped out and tried a new venture. That ability to risk has permitted us to venture into new paths where God is speaking today. We can learn to listen to the inner voice that comes from our souls and leaps into the void that contains the all.

At age thirty-three, what did we have to lose? We were about to have our fourth daughter when we started our new business. We had a nice house, but we felt it was the right thing to do for the future. We knew everything would be fine, and it was. Our new business was with the professional movie industry in New York City. We produced technology that aided in the rapid turnaround of films for the evening news.

All news was on film at that time (1967) as videotape machines had not been introduced. Two years later, the first videotape machine was introduced. All of our clients suddenly feared the loss of their most lucrative business, and our orders vanished.

Shortly after that event, when it was obvious we were not going to make it, I received a call from my previous manager at the television-research organization. They were starting a new research job, and he wanted me to take over the effort. They offered me a great salary—they did not know our problems—and I accepted. I returned to my previous location with a new title, great pay (a 50 percent increase from what I had left two years before), and all was well.

It may look easy to take a risk on a new venture, but what about when problems appear? My wife and I have always chosen to trust. We know that God will guide us through. When I lost my job in 1970, we trusted God would find us sufficient income. That worked out well. When we moved my wife's mother to our home, she developed cancer and died in the midst of a loving family. That was the hidden purpose of her move to our home. When our house burnt completely in 1984, we trusted that God would see us through. And we love our new house.

Trust!

God is there, and we live immersed in the Holy Spirit. That is how God works. We build our own lives with all the ups and downs. We are our own creators, and our choices move us along. We create each 'now' in our lives—in response to the 'now' of one another. We fashion our lives according to the patterns we set. That pattern always matches our deepest desires.

We set that pattern unconsciously—unless we choose to set a conscious pattern in our lives. That forms abundance. That pattern can be forced by methods of self-hypnosis (which usually ultimately fails) or with the trust and knowledge that God will give us only the best for our lives.

The choice is ours.

> ***The world is made of faith,***
> ***And trust,***
> ***and pixie dust.***
> ***—J.M.Barrie. Peter Pan***

Questions to Ponder

When have you been too afraid to take a calculated risk that could have changed your life? Write down the opportunities that you failed to take.

Write down the opportunities you did take and the results.

We build our own lives. How does that make you feel? Do you see the possibility of that statement being true? Write down your thoughts.

Meditation

Eternal Wisdom, open up my heart and being to sense and trust your wisdom in my life. My very existence is a breath of your being. I—made in your image and being of your very essence—have the kingdom of your being within me. I am waiting to see that level. I thank you for this opportunity to open the gates of my heart to your very being, your life, all life, the very fabric of the universe, and the all in all. I bow in awe as I sense the possibilities that flow around and in me. I see the beauty of the universe in all its glory as a reflection of your vastness and glory. It is a glimpse of my own glory in your being, which is contained in my essence.

Teach me to trust in your love for me. All that I do—based upon that trust in your love—will be beneficial in this round of physicality. Open my heart to this possibility, fueled by trust, to grant me my deepest heart's desires.

Chapter 11

The Physical Nature of Abundance

Where two or three are gathered together in my name, I am there with them.
—Matthew 18:20, NIV, combined with NASB

*I*t is fine from a mystical point of view to state that we create our lives, but how does that fit with the reality of the physical presence of our lives?

Quantum Physics

Amazingly enough, quantum physics agrees with the metaphysical approach that we create our own lives. Quantum physics states that nothing exists as we see it except in the now we view it. Before this instance, this now of being, quantum physics states that everything is but a cloud of possibilities—one of which will exist in the now. Which one? It all depends on the measuring device used. In our case, that measuring device is our perception of each moment. All that we see and perceive is effectively being reborn in every now that exists—down to the smallest particle of time that is believed to be around one part in ten to the -43 seconds. That is, a decimal point followed by forty-two zeros and then a one: 0.000000000000000000000 00000000000000000000001 seconds.

This is a result of the dual nature of the smallest parts of matter. All matter is simultaneously a particle and a wave. The energy packet can be a wave front or bonded into a particle. It is one or the other— or even both until measured—depending on the need or measuring device used at the moment. A camera is the most easily used as an example of the dual nature. It takes many particles of light, called photons, to energize a pixel of a camera. A photon is used in all cameras to excite the surface used to detect the number of photons that determined the brightness of that spot. Even more dualistic is that, depending on the wavelength of light (wave nature), the light is directed by color or wavelength sensitive transparent plates to the color neutral detectors that see the directed photons that represent red, green, or blue color (wavelength) light. On digital cameras, the photon nature of light is used to activate the camera detectors (the measuring device) that create the image recorded in units of particles or photons. The three (red, green, and blue) detectors are identical; only the wave frequency of the light directed to each sensor is different. The detectors only see photon particles—not color or wavelength. A photon of red light has identical properties as a photon of blue light. The difference is only detected when the "photon particle" assumes its dual nature of wavelength or a wave with a given distance between crests.

We see the wave nature of light most easily when we look at a rainbow. We see the different colors, caused by the spreading of the wavelength of light, or the wave distance from peak to peak, depending on the color. Red has a longer distance between peaks than green, which has a longer distance between peaks than blue. The colors result from the wave entering the eye where it changes into a photon by the eye receptor or cone, the measuring device, and the photon is converted into an electrical impulse that is transmitted to the brain. The brain decodes the particular receptors by color.

This dual nature is part of all there is in nature. Even more, it has been proven through the high-energy particle accelerators that even beyond the dual nature, all matter resolves in the basic nature of being energy that is captured and bound by interrelationships of force and gravity, attraction of positive nuclei and negative electrons that remain bound by mutual attraction and repulsion. The nuclei and electrons are swirling masses of energy that cannot be completely defined by location and speed since the energy makes them indeterminate by the very nature of its existence. These boundaries are extremely small, and we have no outward perception of these strange properties. They form the truth of nature, thus form the truth of life, and thus form the truth of all that is in the universe.

This very nature forms the potential for abundance. Science makes it very clear that just because something has always been such and such, there may be a small chance that something different may occur. A slight energy shift here or there could change the outcome, and a surprise may occur. What can cause an energy shift? Any outside force produces a corresponding shift in the presentation of the next now. All 'nows' are the result of past energy, and they are impacted by new energies (such as energy fields) that impinge on the structure. They can, and will, produce a shift in the structure.

The brain radiates energy.

Science has proven that our brains are a source of energy. It is possible to measure the radiation being emitted by the brain. Even more important, research is now being conducted where a fine mesh can pick up individual signals. They are being used to control devices and small robots. Eventually they will help those who have lost arms or legs. This marvelous capability will someday permit those who have suffered birth defects, injuries, or strokes to regain control and live reasonably normal lives, moving, walking, and handling the world around them.

Our thoughts emit energy waves that surround us all the time. It does not take a great stretch of imagination to see that these energy waves impact all that we are and all that we do. We all know negative people who are surrounded by doom and gloom in all they see. Usually, everything that happens to them proves them right.

And we know really positive, high-energy folks who draw others to themselves like magnets—for good or bad. Most leaders in groups, business, or politics fit in this pattern. It can be positive (Mother Teresa) or negative (Hitler).

All of us, no matter who we are, think. We radiate energy that reflects who we are—both the good and the bad. The net that is used in brain wave research works on everyone. The energy waves go out into the universe, and that energy is never lost. It continues to travel unless it is absorbed, but it is still present in the higher energy levels of the object that observed

Science without religion is lame, religion without science is blind.
—Albert Einstein

it. The observer field is somehow modified by this new energy. Part goes through everything and joins the general energy level of the universe, but it is still distinct from everything else. We may not have instruments that can measure or distinguish the signals, but the laws of physics state that they are always there, in their own manner, distinct from all else.

Our thinking changes the world.

The radiation levels we emit strike everything and everyone around us. Like any radiation, they affect everything around us in some form. We all know how a negative person puts a damper on an event, and sometimes this happens without any outward sign that we are aware of, but the event did not reach the level it should have. This failure could be caused by extreme negativity of one or more persons.

It works in the opposite manner also. If extremely positive people are present, the event can reach levels totally unexpected in joy and happiness—without any outward sign from anyone, just a level of 'yes' that is felt by all.

We can see how abundance cannot just be a mystical event. It is a physical event that follows the sequence outlined by quantum physics. If we think of a desired outcome, we are influencing our surrounding aura or brain waves that impact and tweak all things around us. If we think of this outcome deeply enough and often enough, it can begin to affect the outcome of what occurs around us. And if we are consistent in our efforts, that desired outcome can become a reality in our lives.

We can be happy and find joy in any circumstance. That is abundance.

Happiness is a warm puppy.
— Charles M. Schulz

Questions to Ponder

Does the fact that physical reality as spelled out by quantum physics agrees with the metaphysical or mystical approach affect your perceived world? Write down your thoughts about this alignment of worlds.

Does this dual thinking produce excitement or fear? Write down your feelings.

"Where two or three are gathered together in my name, I am there with them" (Matt 18:20). How does this fit into this discussion?

Meditation

Thank you, Eternal Wisdom, for this universe that is so responsive to my deepest desires. I find it astounding that what I call abundance is a process of creation, controlled in some manner by my very thoughts and actions, creating an energy that changes everything. This cause (my thinking) and effect (the result) are amazing, defining for me the depth of the meaning to the words of Jesus: *"If you have the faith of a mustard seed, and you tell this mountain to hurl itself into the sea, it will be done."* I stand in awe in the depth of being one with you.

The evolutionary reality of mystical being and physical being is marvelous to behold, and I am excited to be present at this crossroads where I am catch a glimmer of your creative genius in the fullness of our universe. The more I learn, the more I am in awe of the world around me—in the physical reality and the mystical link in this universe.

Humanity seem to know so much, but we have just begun to uncover the unity of science and religion—seemingly to the dismay of both. This unity begins to make sense of everything there is, much like the grand unifying theory that seems just out of reach of science and religion. I am grateful for this opportunity you have granted me.

Chapter 12

Synchronicity

*And it shall come to pass that, before they call,
I will answer; and while they are yet
speaking, I will hear.*
—Isaiah 65:24, NASB, paraphrased

*T*he explanation of the natural features of abundance from the last discussion still does not explain the seemingly impossible features of many occurrences of coincidences or other wonderful events of our lives that defy explanation.

Particularly puzzling are events that come together defying time—where what occurs had to have started long before even the need became a concern or desire. Just as it became apparent that my small company had a serious financial problem, our principle customer unexpectedly came with an order that solved all our problems. It is obvious to me, knowing how large companies operate, that this had been worked on for many months without our knowledge. Where did that come from? How did Providence, Eternal Wisdom, and universal energy flow work that effort? That is a key example of *synchronicity* at work; that is when inexpiable coincidences occur in life.

I suspect you will find many instances when spooky things happened and solved problems in your life. Those happenings are not coincidences. Instead, God (the universal energy flow) nudges to set things as they should be, according to your deepest desires, unknown to you.

God is not limited by time.

God is not limited by time. God works around the linear function of time. God sees all as now, occurring all at once in all the variations possible. We see only the 'now' that is in our time, followed by the next 'now', which is dependent on our response to this 'now', moment by moment. God 'understood' (I do not believe God 'understands' things the way we use the term 'understand') what was occurring at our company, and metaphorically speaking, God foresaw the sequence of 'nows' that understood (knew) the bank's refusal and the ensuing potential consequences. God acted long before to set in motion the process that led to the order just in time.

But just as mystifying is the answer given by quantum mechanics, the theory of possibilities. The theory of relativity, generated by Einstein, which is the mathematical description of the operation of the whole universe, or the macro-world, has a function of time. In the general theory of relativity, energy equals mass times the speed of light squared. The speed of light is measured in kilometers per second. Note the function of time (kilometers per second). The more obscure math functions of quantum physics, which deal with the micro-world and the world of possibilities, has no function of time involved. The implication that is understood by those whose lives are devoted to the study of quantum physics is that it is a distinct possibility that an event experienced in the now can reach back and change events in the past to allow the present now to exist.

A sequence of events is not necessarily linear in time.

This brings all kinds of mind-boggling possibilities. I will not talk about these here since they do not bear on this topic, but it does raise the possibility that time has little to do with the sequence of events that give birth to a particular event. It is a possibility that a series of events reached back in time to trigger the sequence that encouraged the customer to place the order at the needed moment.

Did Eternal Wisdom foresee the sequence of events needed long before it became evident in time and set in motion the sequence?

Which, if either, is true? Does it matter? Both result in the needed actions. Both are correct, and perhaps both are the same. The metaphysical and the physics-based approach state that time is not an obstacle to reach a given result. It may seem strange, but perhaps understanding quantum physics gives us a glimpse of the workings of the mystical world, the world of the Eternal Wisdom, or the way God operates. Is that the working of God? Perhaps this is the time that the eternal workings of the eternal spirit are becoming understandable to the individualizations of God, namely, humanity.

Metaphysics explains the why of science.

The insight between the parallels of the world of quantum physics and the thinking of the metaphysical world reveal no opposition between science and the mystical or metaphysical world. There is an agreement in the basic functioning of the two lines of thought. This agreement is beginning to appear to be consistent, and

> *There are only two ways to live your life. One is as though nothing is a miracle, the other is as though everything is a miracle.*
> *—Albert Einstein*

it points out the possibility that eventually we will be able to understand the mind of God—at least at the edges. As God is made more manifest to us, we will meld more and more into the wisdom of the Eternal Spirit.

This is how it has to be if either thought process is correct. There cannot be any disagreement between these two approaches (religion and physics) to explaining the universe(s) that exist. I have spent sixty years studying both approaches, and I have never seen a true disagreement between the two. There are language differences. Both describe a process of creation. Science gives us facts and a trail to show how these facts both bewilder us and confirm the process of life. The metaphysical approach gives us a why and explains the meaning of the world of science. Where seemingly intractable differences appear, I tend to lean more toward what science says. After pondering and studying more, I find that the "intractable" moment has vanished—and both agree. I have never found a true disagreement that did not reveal how the basic scientific truth bore the truth, both scientifically and metaphysically, of things.

One of principle reasons I prefer the scientific approach is that, unlike the religious approach, science is not afraid to change what it states. Usually the finer results end in subtle changes, but even when great discoveries are made—such as that the earth is not the center of the universe—science moved forward and used that knowledge to understand more and more of the paths of masters and mystics. We can understand the interrelationships of the physical parts of the universe, revealing how all is one in being with

God. We are all one. In fact, as science has shown us, everything is one. There is no real differential between the universe and conscious life as we understand it— and as we will understand further in the future.

Abundance stems out of the basic function of who we are. If we can bring ourselves into alignment with our true natures, our oneness with the All in All, we would understand that what we have is the power of All That Is within us. Nothing is beyond our grasp. All we desire in our souls is within our grasp. We can achieve all that we need. *"Greater things than this shall you do."* To put it in a phrase that abundance can relate, I say, *"Greater things than this shall I do."*

It is ours to deny, ours to resist, ours to say, *"Not me, Lord. Not me, surely! You cannot be asking me to take that role."* It is also ours to accept, ours to demand, and ours to understand that Jesus was talking to you and to me when he said, *"Greater things than this shall you do."* Do we accept the challenge Jesus gives us or lay down your birthright and walk away from the great challenges in life?

Humanity must awaken.

Humanity has reached a critical point in its evolution. We have reached, in sheer numbers and technology, a level that will destroy civilization unless we change our approach to life. Life will not vanish, but life and humanity will have to make drastic adaptations to survive. It could be thousands of years before this level of potential will exist again. I see the potential for a convergence of the spiritual and the scientific that will bring the two to a potential agreement and allow more commonality to be achieved among the various factions that exist. I believe that more of humanity must realize that we cannot continue in this current pattern of ego-driven power. For the sake of survival, we must band together to solve the problems of the world.

I know not with what weapons
World War III will be fought,
But World War IV will be fought
With sticks and stones.
— Albert Einstein

Questions to Ponder

Have you seen moments of undeniable and unbelievable coincidences (moments of synchronicity) in your life?

Write down the moments of synchronicity in your life: meeting your life mate, getting a new job, or starting a wonderful friendship.

How does the thought of awakening to a new level of understanding your conscious metaphysical understanding help in your life journey?

Write down your thoughts on the potential of that journey in the future.

Meditation

I bow in awe, Eternal Wisdom, to your techniques of pushing, tantalizing, suggesting, hinting, and other methods of calling me out of ignorance and fear into enlightenment and joy. Your dual approach of physical hinting and metaphysical hinting draws upon the innate curiosity of humanity and can never be denied. It leads me to a level of understanding that could not happen in any other way. I am in awe at the methods You use to lead me to basic truths—via science, spirituality, and metaphysics. Grant me the wisdom to unite these seemingly diverse paths into a single strand that reveals your truth in the wholeness of creation as You intended.

I have caught glimpses of how these changing insights into the very nature of life itself urges humanity onward to more a common sense of purpose and fulfillment. I am grateful that You have opened up this marvelous world to me, allowing me to taste Your goodness that we are immersed in.

Chapter 13

You Are Worthy of God's Love

The light of God surrounds me,
The love of God enfolds me,
The power of God protects me,
The presence of God watches over me.
Whereas I am, God is.
—Prayer Card

*J*esus said, *"But seek first the Kingdom of God and God's righteousness, and all these things will be given to you as well."* (Matt. 6:13, New Heart English Bible). I call this approach abundance. The most common term tossed around today to gain our heart's desire is prosperity, which denotes material richness. Those teaching prosperity, such as the writings of *The Secret*, talk about wealth and other physical and material gains.

Peace of Mind

I have found that peace of mind and the soul are far more important to life than wealth. Gaining abundance could include wealth as well as peace of mind, but a rich life is filled with peace of mind and self-assurance more than monetary wealth. A nice car is good, a larger home is nice, and a comfortable lifestyle and good health are important, but having all that and not having peace of mind makes life miserable. Robin Williams had everything that could be desired—really big home, fancy cars, fame—but he found life so difficult that he was driven to suicide. How sad.

I have not used the term *prosperity*, but I will use the term *abundance*. I believe, from my experiences, that living a life of abundance results in acceptance of my life as it is right now, is the peak of living a full life—no matter the external conditions.

I have not lived a life of complete abundance (joy and happiness), but my life has been mostly filled with abundance, that is, I was joyful and happy, whether I was fully aware of that fact or not. I was always able to live close to the moment and not be too concerned about the future. I was careful not to indulge too much and kept close track of expenses. After all, raising seven children takes care and a certain amount of planning. We always had a nice house that was large enough for all of us. Right now, we have five bedrooms for the two of us, but even that is not large enough when all come home with families.

The kingdom of God lies within.

Jesus said, *"Seek first the kingdom of God."* After that, he said, *"All these things will be given to you."* I do not believe that Jesus was speaking of physical wealth, big cars, large homes, etc. Jesus was speaking of sufficiency, peace of mind, joy, and happiness.

I have led a very comfortable life, much to my amazement. I did not seek what I now have—even though I dreamed and expected to live comfortably by the time I reached my present age. I have worked all my life, and I finally decided to end my daily involvement with my company at age 80. I suspect it will take me some time to move further away since I own half of the company. I am on the e-mail trail of events, and two of our sons work there. It will take some willpower to prevent myself from becoming more involved than I wish to be.

My wife and I have involved ourselves in our search for God. We were usually satisfied where we were, but we were always looking, listening, praying, and studying to understand God's presence in our lives. We always trusted that God would guide us to the next appropriate spot where we were supposed to share our faith and knowledge with others. We've tried to be a funnel for the Word of God in our world.

The secret is time.

Both of us pray every day. Over the years, the prayers were often short (seven children!), but they were always there. We were aware that God spoke through humans, and we would try to be aware of the working of God in our lives. Sometimes we struggled with life, and sometimes it was hard, but we always spent a few minutes a day immersed in the Holy Spirit.

We knew that God was with us. God was guiding us, pushing us, and sometimes slamming us on the side of the head (or so it seemed) to follow God's path for us. Sometimes the next step would appear just moments before we took the step—or even after

> *It is only by forgetting yourself that you draw near to God.*
> *—Henry David Thoreau*

we had taken the step in blind faith. We always knew that we would be all right. That is confidence in God, and that is the path to abundance, joy, and happiness. Not will-power to keep ones desires central in mind; not writing lists and intense concentration; just the confidence in the Will of God to see us happy, to exercise God's Love as revealed to us, to ride the Love of God in every moment.

God, in the form of the universe, gives us precisely what lies in our heart. That sounds faulty since so much of our lives can be difficult, but what thoughts or feelings are deep in our hearts? This is the key to abundance. Do we believe that we do not have it and must pray to have it in the future? I have discovered the truth that if we believe we do not have it right now, in the deepest part of our hearts, then we will not have it in the next now. The universe works to satisfy our deepest thoughts. It always satisfies our deepest beliefs about who we are. If we believe we are not worthy of the blessings of God, we will fail to achieve our goals.

The universe creates.

The secret of the universe is that it always gives us what we believe—not what we spout and not what we think. Our deepest beliefs must hold to truth: I am worthy. One of the greatest disservices our religions have foisted upon us is that we are not worthy. God *"made humanity in God's own image, in God's image they made them"* (Genesis 1:27, New Heart English Bible, paraphrased). Our religions have pounded into us that we are not worthy, ignoring that we are made in the very image of God. Since we believe we are not worthy, we cannot believe that God really loves us. But the truth is, God grants us anything we desire and believe about ourselves.

I am worthy of the love of God.

I always knew that I am worthy and that God really loves me. God can make anything happen in a form that is the very best for me at that stage of my life. This level of trust in God is the goal if abundance is to be a firm part of your life.

Whatever is going on, all will be well. All will be well!

You must believe that you are worthy. I must believe that I am worthy. It does not matter what I did. It does not matter how much I have strayed. I am worthy because I am made in the image of God. Nothing else matters. You are worthy because you and God are one. You have the same ability to achieve everything. We are limited by what we believe—not by what may occur. Jesus said, *"Greater things than this shall you do."* Jesus preceded that with *"if you have the faith of a mustard seed"* (Matt. 17:20, ESV). How do we deny what is so clear? Too much of our religions do not want us to understand that we have the capacity to do all that Jesus said we could do if we have the faith of the mustard seed.

If we have faith and the knowledge that we are worthy, we can achieve anything we deeply desire: – to be filled with a sense of joy and happiness is our deepest desire. Are we ready to try that approach? Much of our religions do not really want us to do that, but are you willing to try that approach? This is the road that the mystics took, and it took them to sublime heights. This road can do the same for you.

The bliss of God awaits you.

God has no religion
—Mahatma Gandhi

Questions to Ponder

Do you feel worthy in your heart of entering the "kingdom of God within" your heart?

Write down how that question makes you feel.

Does the bliss of God seem possible in your life?

Write down your heartfelt thoughts about the statement that God is just waiting for your acceptance of God's love to unlock the key to joy and happiness.

Meditation

O Holy Wisdom, you have given me the gift of yourself, which ensured that all I believe is mine. I bow in gratitude for these marvelous gifts, these perfect gifts, for all that I have which reflect all I believe about myself. You have blessed us with beauty in our lives, from the breathtaking beauty of the newborn child to the fluttering butterfly to the sighing breeze to the majestic mountains to the thundering seas. Truly I live in paradise, and your kingdom envelops me. Help me open my eyes as I see the unfolding events of my life and see the perfection within—from birth to death. Thank you for helping me see your wonders of life as I see your perfection in all.

Chapter 14

Acceptance

*I accept life unconditionally...
most people ask for life on condition.
Happiness can only be felt if
You don't set any conditions.
—Arthur Rubenstein*

A cceptance is one of the key points for obtaining abundance: acceptance of life, acceptance of circumstances, and acceptances of events in life. Acceptance in life does not mean giving up on anything or giving in to all.

Acceptance is accepting each circumstance and event in your life as a given, and since it is in the past, it cannot be changed. Accept and take the next step, as best as you can see it, to move toward a positive goal.

We govern our lives.

For acceptance to be most effective, one realizes that each event is the result of our inner desires. What has happened in the past—our mental and physical being—is the best it can be and serves a purpose in life. We are where we are because we know that these events will lead us to our purpose.

This level of faith, at least that of a mustard seed, is the key to abundance at any level. This level of faith is needed to *"do greater than this,"* as Jesus said. Faith is the dimension of our lives and reaches into our souls. It provides the link to the soul that can join awareness, our deepest spirit, and our souls—where the infinite being that we are is centered. Our souls understand and hold purpose for our lives. We were born to venture into this round of creation. That is why we left the core of God to know who we are.

Life is good.

The greatest benefit that occurs in acceptance of our lives as it occurs is that we understand that life is always good. It provides the best that can happen to us for our inner peace and rest. Nothing is wrong or misplaced, and each event leads us to fulfill our purpose.

God has no plan for our lives, but we do have a purpose in life. How we fill that purpose, what plan we follow, is our choice. We are never forced to follow a predetermined plan. The next step we take is always a result of the step we just took. Usually it is a simple move with few choices, but sometimes we make a choice that leads to totally a different path. Either path would have resulted in a set of choices that would meet our purpose, but taking the choice we did firmed up the choices.

Choices, Choices

When I chose to go to school to be an engineer, it set a course for my entire life. When I chose to take the job on Long Island rather than accepting the PhD program at Ohio State, it led to a whole different set of choices. Each of us has had a series of choices; some choices may have been better than others, but each choice led to other choices. If you are married or have a significant other, the choices that led to your meeting led to your being together today. The choice to join a group, attend a party, or go to an event led to making the acquaintance of that person. You had to make the choice of bonding that led to your being together.

If we allow ourselves to think about all the choices we've made, it is amazing that we lead the lives we live. Life is a series of events that can be richer or poorer for us, leading to richer events or destructive behavior.

Everything we really accept undergoes a change. So suffering must become love. That is the mystery.
—Katherine Mansfield

It will all serve the purpose of our souls in this round of creation or incarnation.

God will always provide the best for us, and the Divine Wisdom will always give us the potential for peace of mind and soul. During the transition of events, it can be painful, but God will not let us down. Every step leads to the result that is best for us if we have faith and courage to choose that which we know is right. We will be happy and peaceful—no matter what signs others see.

Choose your heart.

Acceptance requires us to have that faith to move with the flow. When I made the choice to accept the job on Long Island, I knew the move was the best for me. I was moving seven hundred miles from where I had grown up—away from all I knew. I felt that I was pulled to stretch myself into doing something new. I consulted no one—just my heart. I knew I had to step into the total unknown if I was to reach my best and fulfill my potential.

Did I understand my decision as I just described it at that time? No way! In fact, it was only while writing this that I received the insight that allowed me to understand my decision fifty-eight years ago. That decision came out of my soul—my inner consciousness—where I knew what I had to do. That was my Eternal Wisdom speaking to me through my inner feelings, the core of my being.

Stretch

That stretching brought me into contact with people I would never have known without stepping into the unknown. Most of all, I would not have met the love of my life more than fifty-six years ago. I fell in love with her at first sight, but I had to move seven hundred miles to find that one. She had to walk across the street to where we met. I would not have had the learning opportunities with some of the greatest engineers of the time. I would not have had the opportunity to lead and work in strong movements within the Roman Catholic Church. I would not have had the opportunity to start my own business with a partner I have now known more than forty years and have some of the greatest times of my professional and personal life.

And that is how our lives evolve. We stretch and sometimes step blindly forward to accept what is and reach for what could be. I realize now that the level of stretching required to make that jump was critical to me as a person. I had to move away from the strong influences that surrounded me in my hometown and enter a new atmosphere where no one knew me so I could be the person I believed I was—and not being the person someone else thought I was. I had grown and stretched so much in college; returning to my birthplace would have turned me back into the shy person most thought I was. Only by stretching and going to a new place could I take my newfound self-confidence and ability to its potential.

We learn to accept what is. I understand that I am over eighty and have a limited span ahead. I have a lower physical capacity than I once had, and it will not get better. I have learned to accept that my love has some physical limitations that prevent her from certain activities. Accepting it will allow us to find greater joy in the activities we have, finding joy in life.

Accept

We can moan about circumstances or accept them and see what is the best we can do. That is life. Acceptance is the key to moving on and accomplishing the next thing in our paths. We have choices. Do we take a risk when it is presented—or do we defer? Our choices form our lives. My wife and I are willing to take a risk at this age. We have lived all our lives like that, talking about the possibilities and the place where we are at the moment. Being willing to take a risk, knowing God will not let us down, assures us that it will always be positive and will lead us to the next blessed event. Acceptance assures us that the result will always be a positive experience—even when it is time to transition to the next phase of life.

Death will be a great adventure. It is difficult for the one left behind, bringing sorrow and pain, but my love and I are joined for eternity. Our love has been honed by more than fifty-six years of life. This love will not diminish, no matter how often we get on each other's nerves. It still happens, as both of us are full of life, and these events provide the spice of life that leads to more richness of being. We are one being, and we understand that life is to be lived without regret or wishing something else had occurred. Our life has occurred with all the choices we have made.

God is good. Life is good. God and life are one in being and one in living.

> *"Many of us crucify ourselves*
> *Between two thieves =*
> *Regret for the past*
> *And fear of the future."*
> *— Fulton Ousler*

Questions to Ponder

Can you accept what life has handed you up to this point in your life? Does your life haunt you with events and choices that are still painful?

Write down your answers that swell from the heart.

What are some of the choices you made that changed your whole life? Think of marriage choices, career, etc.

Write down some of the major choices you made. What has been the impact these choices?

Meditation

Eternal Wisdom, I am grateful for all that you have offered me in my lives. I have tried to live a life of exuberance, one filled with truth and joy, filled with your presence, and I have succeeded beyond my wildest dreams. You have taught me acceptance and knowledge that all is good, that life is good. Your presence fills me with joy. *"The kingdom of God lies within and about me,"* and I thank you and have great gratitude for allowing me to see that kingdom that is there in life.

Chapter 15

Abundance: Our Choice

*Each of us makes their own weather,
Determines the color of the skies,
In the emotional universe
which they inhabit.*
—Fulton J. Sheen

We have talked about the nature of abundance, both from a natural and an esoteric approach. These approaches began to show us that we control the engine of life, that the results can be a life filled with abundance, joy, peace of mind, and happiness— or disaster. Our lives can have good times, health, and wealth or lean times, illness, and poverty. They can be a mishmash of both sides of the coin. Outward appearance is only part of the story; it all depends on how we see life and the perspective we bring to our lives.

We are the authors of our lives.

We control much of the destiny of our lives. We are the engines of our lives, bringing our energies to the creative process we work with in each moment of our lives. We are the authors of our lives—from a spiritual approach to life and a quantum physical approach to life.

Jesus reminds us that our lives are up to us. What we have faith in will occur. Quantum physics says that our thinking and beliefs intersect with all the possibilities to produce the next moment and our energies affect the results. Additionally, our perspective on each moment creates the next moment in our minds, which always leads to the next moments in our life.

We are the engines of our lives. What we do and what happens in our lives are a combination of the places we find ourselves in, our perspectives on life, and how we feel about life in a given moment. Our life experiences are a product of our beliefs and fundamental understanding of life. What we believe in our very beings, our gut feelings, is what occurs in our lives.

Yes, we are the engines of our lives. What we believe is true is what is true for us, but that belief is deep in our soul and is not a function of our surface thoughts.

My belief is what is so in my life.

I have led a life of abundance because I believe I have led a life of abundance. As I see my life, one great thing has led to the next great thing. There were speed bumps in the road on occasion, but life has been one glorious run of joy and abundance. We have had abundance in the midst of clinical depression, abundance when out of a job, abundance when we were struggling to put children through college, abundance when our parents or immediate family passed, and abundance in everything. We always had what we needed to get through the moment. In the end, we have had the peace that passes all understanding.

The Faith of a Mustard Seed

As we believed it, it was so—just as Jesus promised. Jesus said: "If you have the faith of a mustard seed, you can say to this mountain move from here to there, it will move. Nothing will be impossible to you." Matt 17:20, ESV.

Nothing will be impossible to you!

Few of us believe that tantalizing phrase of Jesus.

A life of abundance, filled with joy and happiness, is ours for the taking. We have talked about this from a spiritual point of view and the physical viewpoint of quantum physics. Too many believe that our lives are totally preordained and that Fate controls everything that occurs to us. No matter what we desire or try in life, Fate grabs us by the scruff of the neck and jams us into the next ill-fitting suit or dress. There we are—despite all we try.

But: We have the ability to move mountains—as Jesus said.

Most of the time, we do not believe we have the ability to move mountains. We believe, deep in our being, that *we do not have that ability*, and life responds to our beliefs. Life occurs as an interplay between all that surrounds us, and it is a result of the battles between the strongest of wills, passing thoughts, whims, and life as it rolls.

We *can* be the engines of our lives. I will make a bold statement:

> ***We are the engines of our own lives.***
> ***We design the lives we live.***
> ***We can control our lives***
> ***If we understand the process.***

My life illustrates the wonders of this process. I did not set out to do this in life, but I was given the gift of faith in childhood. I was given unconditional love, and that is part of the gift of life. Saying "Life" is equivalent to saying "God". God and Life are the same. Speaking of God is speaking of life, and speaking of life is speaking of God. Nothing that is of God is not full of life—and nothing that is life is not full of God.

God is always eager to give us all we desire as part of life. Nothing we desire is denied. All prayers are answered as we state them in our hearts. It is somewhat tricky, but the results are always perfect and true. Nothing is impossible. Do you believe that statement? Did you ever believe it? Nothing is impossible! Nothing! But it does take the faith of a mustard seed.

We are the creators of our lives.

We create our lives, based on the starting points we have chosen. The lives we find ourselves in right now are the result of all the various truths we have held over the years (good and bad). Sometimes that faith is high, but we usually let faith drift in the winds of the ins and outs of life. That is the fodder that gives our lives possibilities. These ins and outs provide the means to move into abundance with a change in mind-set. Could this be the start of abundance? Are we blinded to the possibility of what is there?

> *It takes courage to lead a life. Any life.*
> *—Erica Jong*

Anything we see, anyplace we are, and all the circumstances we see could be the start of abundance if we see it as abundance.

Can it be that simple? No way, we say. "It can't be that simple. Much more must be involved". But abundance is ours for the taking, but we only if see that what lies before us is abundance. We believe that in our hearts that God is good.

If you have the faith of a mustard seed, nothing is impossible.

*"The way to get started
Is to quit talking
And begin doing."*
—The Walt Disney Co.

Questions to Ponder

Do you believe you are the author of your life?

Write down your feelings about this statement.

If you could change the direction of your life, would you?

Write down your thoughts about this.

Meditation

God surrounds me, infuses me, is my very being. I look with gratitude at the gift of faith that you have offered me. I have the capability to place myself in your being, to let you flow though me and be present in all that I am. You have shown me over and over that I am made in your image and likeness in all things. This discovery awes me, opens up the sacred to me, and gives me the possibility that heaven on earth exists within and around me. Jesus said, *"The kingdom of God lies within you."* I sigh in love and gratitude at the vision you have given me in this earth. The universe gives me glimpses of your being.

I bow before your words and open my heart to this possibility. Nothing is impossible.

Chapter 16

Nothing Is Impossible

I am the engine of my life
I design the life I live.
I can control my life
If I but understand the process.

This startling statement is a direct result of thinking esoterically and thinking from a quantum physics viewpoint. Jesus said, *"If you have the faith of a mustard seed, nothing is impossible."* This wild statement is hardly ever taken as it was spoken—nothing is impossible.

Hardheaded "realists," as they term themselves, laugh at this and call it childish or the voice of a dreamer. They point out all the calamities of everything around us, but we see the small miracles of life and the impossible miracle of life itself. If we think just a bit, maybe there is at least some truth in those words, *"Nothing is impossible."* The double helix of the DNA strand evolved from a world that the realists state is collapsing into the stasis of nothing (entropy). Energy can never be gained or lost; it is only converted from active higher-energy state to a lower-energy state. The excess energy is lost to electromagnetic energy to wander the universe.

Science agrees that nothing is impossible.

Many of those in science have come to believe that life abounds in our universe even though we have yet to discover life outside of our planet. Despite intensive research, we do not know how life began on earth. One of the more interesting parts of life on earth that everything that has life has a DNA strand which contains the same parent DNA – only one parent DNA exists on earth, from the smallest single cell life to humanity.

The constant drive by the universe to greater complexity, culminating in the complexity of DNA, gives us a look at the working of the universe. From all signs, it is evolving to greater and greater complexity. Science has viewed this with mixed feelings and wonderment. It goes against traditional thinking using entropy, but it fits with the theory that life responds to the pressure of a changing environment. This too goes against the mainstream Darwinian theory of purely random changes has made all the various forms of life we see. A more complex approach has better odds of survival in a hostile environment because more complex systems can self-organize differently under environmental stresses (not only random) than simple systems, and self-organizing systems produce the adaptability for life.

This fits with the quantum knowledge of the past century. All thinking about how matter came to be and even the very nature of the universe came to be called into question. The breathtaking evolution of thinking in a quantum fashion, combined with the mind-twisting insights gained from Einstein's relativity research, has thrown all of science into a tailspin. When viewed with an open mind, the words of Jesus make sense: *"Nothing is impossible."* When we study these massive breakthroughs in scientific thinking, we understand that 'nothing is impossible'.

This is most easily seen from the quantum viewpoint. The mathematics of the very small states very strange things, including that time does not exist in the very small world of quantum mechanics—as strange as that seems. In this strange world, nothing is real until it is observed. Nothing exists until 'now'. Before that, only possibilities exist. Before this observation in the 'now' occurs, it could be 'this' or it could be 'that'. Due to the multiplicity of observers, there is very little difference between 'this' and 'that'. There is always the possibility of a shift in the 'now', resulting in a new 'this' for you or me. This new 'this' will be different from the 'that' that could have been, but for a difference in the energy of observation made by the observer. If we change our energy of observation, something new will occur. It will head in a slightly different direction to something different than if we had started with a different energy level.

This may seem complicated, but it is simplicity itself. Science says that the observer changes what is observed. This is what occurs when a rainbow appears. The moisture content separates and bends the rays of light according to the wavelength of the individual energy of the light. If treated as a particle, it would just move straight on, but in the dual nature of a broad front wave, it spreads out and we see the beauty of a rainbow. It is a spread of the energy level of the individual photon. A photon particle of a given energy has a certain corresponding wavelength in the field mode of existence. If it has a higher energy, it has a shorter ("bluer") wavelength. Before observation, that bit of energy exists in *both* the particle and the field modes of existence.

The Dual Nature of the Universe

An experiment that has been duplicated many times proves the dual nature of light. A sensitive film or sensor is placed behind a plate with a very small space from the plate to the film or sensor. A film or sensor cannot detect energy waves; it only detects a photon particle. The plate contains two small holes. A single photon particle of light is shot from a source controlled to emit one photon particle at a time, upon command. It was aimed at the space between the holes, and this is proved by placing the film or sensor in that space. When tested, the photon lands in the center—between the two holes—every time. Nothing should have passed through the two holes since the photon particle was aimed at the space between. But when the film or sensor *behind the plate* is developed, the single photon is imaged on the film or sensor at exactly the center of the space between the two holes, proving that the light became a wave front, passed through both of the two holes, and then became a photon particle when it struck the sensor or film in the center on the other sides.

The cause? The "observation point" was the film on the other side. The light could be both a particle and a wave until measured by the film on the other side since no observation had determined the state until the film or sensor. The film only responds to photon particles; the film has no knowledge of the wave nature of a photon in a film. This event had been seen long before quantum theory was formed, and it was one of the great mysteries of science—until quantum theory emerged and explained that nothing is firm until it is observed. The dual nature of light has been expanded to include all matter. The matter we see and love only comes into existence when now occurs to give the probability nature of matter the form we observe.

Nothing is impossible.

Nothing is impossible with God.

Did Jesus know about quantum theory? No, he was a product of his own time. But he did understand something far more important than quantum theory. He understood that the workings of the universe is a product of the wisdom of God, that nothing was impossible with God, and that the universe is able to create anything if the correct type of energy is directed at that item.

Jesus understood that nothing is impossible from an esoteric viewpoint. This viewpoint is just as valid as a scientific viewpoint since science is just bringing out the workings of the universe in a manner that can be understood and used in a fashion to evolve the world to become what was the intention of God during the creation of the universe 13.7 billion years ago. Science is beginning to explain, in a mathematical manner, the underpinnings of the wonder of fabric of the universe and the fabric of the workings of God.

This path of understanding of the working of the fabric of God is a step in the process of changing humanity in the next step of conscious evolution. We can choose to evolve to the next level, to know and taste God in all we do. It is possible, and we will hopefully reach that level of consciousness before we destroy ourselves in the process. Right now, we understand that we have the means to affect our personal lives and the lives of those around us.

Nothing is impossible, according to Jesus and science.

Having the faith of a mustard seed disclosed the means of achieving our desires and goals in life. Faith, belief, and absolute certainty are needed to bring to life the power to "move the mountain from here to there." Achieving that level of faith is a process that will take some discussing and some effort. A life filled with abundance is possible and easily obtained.

Faith is the means of modifying the observation to achieve our goals in life. Science says that the observer modifies the event, and the implication is that the energy exuded by the observer is the modifying force. The element of faith is the key to bringing about the internal objective of life—to attain joy and happiness—despite what appears to be happening in life. The key is finding that source of faith that we can draw upon to obtain the foundation of knowing that the result will be knowledge that the result of the 'now' will always be perfect for us to achieve our real goals in life. We will understand who we are, why we are, and the purpose of our lives.

We are unique. We are the only one who can achieve our purposes. We are here to reach that goal. It is not elusive; it is a result that can be reached if we let ourselves reach out with the faith of a mustard seed. You are reading this because you have been given the grace to reach this level of understanding. You exist in this here and now—no matter if you are young or old. Reaching the next level of understanding of the universe is only a matter of a switch of perspective. It requires no time—just a change in thought patterns.

> *"Ah, it is impossible."*
> *"No, it is only very difficult –*
> *So very difficult I shall*
> *Be sure to accomplish it."*
> *E.D.E. N. Southworth, Capitola's Peril*

Questions to Ponder

Do you sense the potential that you may be able to move mountains and find joy and peace in your life?

Write down your feelings on the possibility of finding peace and joy.

Both science and wisdom state that we have the power to change our perspectives. Does this thought empower you to respond?

Write down any thoughts that come to you about the potential to respond to this calling for all humanity.

Meditation

Holy Spirit, the universe of all, the All in All, I bow in gratitude for guiding me in this path of understanding your will in this life and beyond. Thank you for this opportunity to understand your presence and the purpose of my life during this experience of life. I see the evolving universe and understand that I am a part of the evolving process of life. I swim in the mysterious ways of evolution—understanding only the surface—and marvel at the interplay between science and the esoteric world. I sigh in bliss at being granted the chance to join more fully from my heart to see the interplay of the universe and my life. The potential to join in the ever-flowing pattern of the universe and sing songs of joy that fill everything is overwhelming. It brings hope to my being that I may see the heaven that lies within.

Chapter 17

The Faith of a Mustard Seed

If you have the faith of a mustard seed,
You could say to a mountain:
Move from here to there, and it would.
Nothing would be impossible to you.
—Matthew 17:20, ESV

If you have no doubt (the faith of a mustard seed), nothing is impossible. As we briefly discussed last time, science says the same thing. The odds of realizing (and using that knowledge) that anything is possible is still a matter of statistics, with some things fairly easy to move toward, and some things are extremely difficult.

The most quoted example of that in scientific literature is a discussion of the air in a given room. Since the molecules of the gas of air are always moving, colliding, and moving in a new random direction, there is a chance that all the molecules could move to one corner of the room, leaving a perfect vacuum in the rest of the room. Mathematicians love to quote the odds of that happening, and it is *extremely* small, but the fact remains that it could happen.

Not Faith, But Knowing

Jesus talked about faith, and his words are very similar to my discussions on the potential of the move of all of the air in a room to a corner of the room. Jesus's powerful words about the mustard seed were spoken as a bit of a putdown to the apostles—they had tried to heal someone, and they wondered why it failed—but they were true. There is always a possibility that a sequence of events could happen—no matter how slim the chance.

Jesus said, "If you had faith." Science says, "If your energy stream is sufficiently powerful." They agree that anything can happen. We are not talking about a machine making energy. We are talking about the energy released by thoughts, will, and conscious control.

The faith that Jesus was talking about was not just a wishful thinking that something would be so and so. I suspect the Aramaic word that Jesus actually spoke was much more intense than our understanding of the word *faith*. Faith, as it is usually understood and practiced, is a nebulous belief that so-and-so is probably true. Very seldom does it reach the level of certitude, and hardly ever does it reach the level of knowing that something will occur. Jesus was talking about a level of absolute certainty ("without doubt") that the healing being requested was already granted, and the person would be healed.

Jesus just knew.

A reading of the healing miracles of Jesus makes that point clearly. He knew that when he looked at a person, he or she was healed at that moment. Jesus spoke, sometimes announcing that when he uttered prayers, he was doing it for those listening—not to plead for the cure but to announce the cure. The cure was already completed, so firm was the faith or knowledge Jesus had.

Jesus, being human and physical, had to work through the process just as any human would have. As physics tells us, if sufficient energy is directed in certain manners, chosen results will occur. Where did that energy come from in the case of Jesus? It came from his thoughts and his will. The result Jesus was looking for occurred. Jesus understood that he, and he alone, controlled his destiny. What he focused on occurred—just as he knew it would. This was not wishing or hoping. This occurred exactly as he saw it, giving the results that were expected. He could turn his attention to something else immediately since the task was already completed in his mind.

Humans have often proven a similar effect. In the so-called placebo effect, half the subjects receive a real drug and half receive a sugar pill. The typical results are amazingly close; typically 40 percent are helped by the drug, and 30 percent helped by the sugar pill. When the blood samples are analyzed, those helped by sugar pill will often have traces of the drug in their bloodstream, indicating that the body manufactured the drug on its own! The belief of the person created the result. That is having the belief of a mustard seed.

And it was so.

Jesus said, *"Greater things than this shall you do"* (John 14:12-14, ESV). Jesus understood the power of the mind and soul—when combined with the focusing capability of the brain-mind-soul—could enable all of us to be capable of directing our lives in a manner to bring the kingdom of God to reality.

We have this capacity, which was spoken of by Jesus and strongly suggested by quantum physics. Our problem has been that we do not believe it. As Jesus suggested, we lack the faith that the words can possibly be true. We hope they are true. We wish they were true. But we have niggling doubts about how they can be true.

Jesus said they were and that we can do these things. Why do they not happen? Why are our lives so fouled up?

We receive exactly what we ask for.

The world gives us exactly what we wish for. Quantum physics makes it clear that the observer determines the results. The results are not happenstance; they are directed by the observing force to reach a conclusion determined by the force upon the potential of each moment.

God, through the pen of Neale Donald Walsch, has talked about this aspect. He states that we receive exactly what we believe. If we *wish* for a given result, a wish is what we get since we know we do not have that result right now, and it would be nice to receive it. That is, if we know that we do not have something and ask to receive it, then we get exactly what we know in our hearts: that we lack such and such. Asking for something is always in the future, and the future never arrives. It is always in the future. And this agrees exactly with quantum physics!

The subjects of the drug test that received the placebo also believed they were receiving the drug, and it responded just as they were told the drug would react—even having the side effects they were told to watch for.

We direct our own energies.

The energy we impart with our souls and minds is very powerful, and it weaves the world around us exactly as we command it be woven. We are the observers of our universe, and an infinite range of possibilities exists in each moment. We are the ones to choose the outcome, like a choose-your-own-adventure book.

We choose our stories.

We write our lives every day. If we do not like our lives, we can choose another path. We have that freedom, but we live with the path and the results we have woven with our previous decisions.

A friend of mine had many problems. He was kicked out of the service for smoking pot, dropped out of college, began drinking too much, got his girlfriend pregnant, got seriously in trouble with the law, and was forced to take some serious looks at himself. He looked very hard (he had lots of help and a loving and supporting family) and decided not to continue that life. He has not had a drink since then, he has a very responsible job, he married his girlfriend, and he is living a reasonably good life. He still has his past record, and he cannot remove those parts that were painful, but those mistakes made him the man he is today, and he acknowledges that fact.

He chose to change his story, and he is sticking to that thread of life. We are as we believe we are. He has changed, and all around him, events have moved to a much more positive light. That is the power of the soul-mind focusing on the path. God has always blessed him and kept the positive force there—even when times were really bad. When he was ready to receive the gifts of God, they just flowed into him.

"Whatever the mind can conceive
And believe, it can achieve."
—Napoleon Hill, Think and Grow Rich: A
Black Choice

Questions to Ponder

Does the potential of being able to write your own story excite you or bring you fear?

Does the fact that you do write the story of your life anger you or challenge you to the point of denial? Do you leap for joy at the chance to change your life? Write down your response.

Meditation

Infinite Knowledge, Spinner of the Universe, Gentle Lover, I allow myself to sigh in bliss in your arms. When I have placed my lives in difficult times, I know that you are present as part of my very being, my soul, to bring me consolation, joy, and happiness. I give myself over to my very being in this existence and relax in your embrace. I am learning to be as Jesus told me, to expand my very being to be a bringer of the light, to accomplish greater things than this. I bow in gratitude for this chance of life, to rise to meet the possibilities you have granted me during this brief passage in physicality.

I ask that you continue to open my hearts to see the kingdom of God that exists all around me, and to continue to enrich my courage as I grow into who I really am in this life of physicality.

Chapter 18

Change Your Perception, Change Your Life

Ask and it will be given to you,
Seek and you will find,
Knock and the door will be opened to you.
—Matthew 7:7, Luke 11:9, NIV

We will examine the potential thought that the statement "Nothing is impossible" could be real. Mathematicians and quantum theoreticians state that in theory that nothing is impossible, but to be practical, everybody agrees that we can expect things to follow a natural course and plod along as expected—except when they do not.

The renowned physicist Steven Hawkins was diagnosed at twenty-two with Lou Gehrig's disease, or ALS, and given two years to live. He is now in his seventies, quite immobilized, but he is still able to think and come up with ideas on the genius level about how the universe came into existence following the laws that control the movements of the universe. Once he accepted who he was, he began treating his illness as a part of life. He continues focus on his work. He is able to concentrate on things other than his illness and the problems the illness has caused in his life. He appears to be able to control the progress of the disease through his will and by focusing on other things.

Will. Focus. Faith.

Will. Focus. Faith. All of these items really result from a "singleness of purpose." In the deepest part of our being, we can learn to come to understand that nothing has to be what it appears to be at the moment. We can shift direction and accomplish something new, something we dared only dream about in the past.

Jesus called it the faith of a mustard seed, but the faith Jesus talked about can only be faith. It has no sizes, so "the faith of a mustard seed" is the "faith of an oak tree." It is mighty and strong, able to withstand any buffet from time or events. Faith becomes something new: knowledge. Jesus showed the same knowledge when he cured someone or raised someone from the dead.

Knowing the Yes of God

Jesus said, *"Your Father knows what you need before you ask"* (Matt 6:8, NIV). *"Ask and it will be given to you, seek and you will find, knock and the door will be opened to you"* (Matt 7:7, Luke 11:9, NIV).

We are dealing with the creator of our universe, the ability to create black holes, stars, galaxies, and dreams. Jesus really understood what faith is all about. It is not hoping; it is *knowing!* It is not desperate wanting; it is moving to the point where the various phrases from Jesus become a foundation in our lives. We build all we have around them, especially when all evidence shows otherwise.

How do we shift perception?

But how do we arrive at the point where we can live the life Jesus promised? The change in direction of the discussion starting below may seem to contradict all I have been saying, but it forms the basis of arriving at the point where we can become that "person of the faith of a mustard seed."

Alcoholics Anonymous, the famous twelve-step program, is based on this very premise.

> *"Step 1: We admitted we were powerless over alcohol—that our lives had become unmanageable."*

"Step 2: We came to believe that a power greater than ourselves could restore us to sanity."

"Step 3: We made a decision to turn our will and our lives over to the care of God as we understood God."

Those in physical addictions have had their bodies betray them. They find themselves in a life of slavery to a substance (alcohol, drugs) or action (gambling, sex) that is slowly killing them. They find themselves unable to function. These first three steps of AA—and the remaining nine—form a means to move the body and its needs out of the way to let in the soul and begin a healing process of the body and mind. If one is in the midst of addictive behavior, I highly recommend the original twelve-step program, including meetings, fellow travelers, and all twelve steps as originally stated. Only when the body has been healed can we move to the shift I am talking about and gain the abundant life. Indeed, many in the 12 step programs are living in joy and happiness, or the abundant life.

The first three steps form the basis of the core steps of faith that we have been talking about. The remaining nine steps outline the methodology of the twelve-step program. First, I will talk about the type of faith needed to achieve the point of total direction of our lives—the achievement of abundance—irrespective of the outward symbols of our lives.

Step 1 says we have a problem and our lives are out of control. For the alcoholic, it is alcohol. We all have problems that haunt us and give us grief at times. For some, it is habits or actions that have caused deep trouble. It is easy to take the twelve steps, adjust them a bit to fit our

Faith dares the soul to go further than it can see.
—William Clarke

circumstances, use them as a means to create a better life, and start a life of faith and joy that brings internal peace and happiness. Many have done this, and I have used the twelve-step approach to shift my life in new directions when habits were threatening me with disaster.

For others, it is actions that have happened to them. Here we see illness, desertion of a spouse, physical, verbal, or mental abuse, or loss of a job. Any of these events can overwhelm us at moments, and we do not see a way out of the morass that seems to be digging deeper and deeper. This latter arrangement is harder to equate to the twelve-step program, but the keys lie in looking at the first three steps and seeing their insights and the shift that is required to face any problem that life throws at us.

I believe it is easy to see where certain events leave us powerless. A spouse has died; how do I handle that? A child has died, became incapacitated, or is seriously ill; how do I handle that? A spouse has been cheating, and the marriage is doomed; how do I handle that? I have been abused physically or mentally; how do I handle that? I have a life-threatening illness or am becoming weak and aging; how do I handle that? My children are reacting to any of those situations; how do I handle that? I seem to be caught in the hands of fate with little or no control over my life; how do I handle that?

Sometimes it is not clear what is causing our sadness, or it feels like something is missing. We may know something is missing, but we cannot point to it. That is fine. An inner sense understands what is going on, and we need to find a way to rely on a sense of balance to find the joy and peace that God has promised us.

Step by Step, One Step at a Time

I will be adjusting the twelve steps to take into account the means to adjust to these situations and find abundance—a life of joy and happiness—as we work through these problems, using the power of our own creation to lift ourselves to the joy of the Eternal One.

1. We admit to ourselves that we are seemingly powerless over our ego.

Put your pain in this place. See yourself in this powerless point. Admit it. Do not let this go. This is the crucial point to moving to faith beyond that of a mustard seed. Admitting that you cannot do it alone is the most critical point required to achieve the faith that can move mountains. It is possible, but we can see that we—in an egoic state—cannot do this on our own. Our egoic life is in shambles and carries a shadow of sadness or restlessness. We have seen ourselves from the ego center, which can never satisfy in the long run. Often we cannot pin the problem to any one thing, and at that point, we can add our voices to all of humanity: My life is a mess.

2. We came to believe that a power greater than the ego could restore us to sanity.

This is the critical point. Do you believe that a power greater than the egoic center can help you get to the point of internal peace? Can you admit that you cannot do it in your separated space? Only the power of God—combined with our joining with that power—has the ability to change the logical outcome. We and God are one. We are an individualization of the Eternal Power and the power that Jesus said was ours to take. *"Greater things than this shall you do."* We have forgotten who we are. That is the only problem. Jesus said: *"The glory which You gave given Me I have given them, that they may be one, just as we are one. I in them and You in Me, that they may be perfected in unity, so that the world may know that You sent Me, and loved them, even as You have loved Me."* (John 17:21, NIV). What more do we want to hear? God told us in many ways that the power to change all is ours for the taking. We only need remember.

3. We made a decision to turn our wills and our lives over to the care of God as we understood God.

The hard part is surrendering ourselves to the power that surrounds us. It fills us and is our internal vital core. Dare we let go and let God? The power of God is ours for the taking. Do we dare? Can we turn our will over to that power and let that power become ours? The eternal power of the Creator is ours for the asking, but we have to ask. We let ourselves fall into that power. There is no holding back. It's time to let go. Let God.

The steps and processes that we will be talking about in the future will be based on our willingness to part with our egoic self. The pride center is the part of you that says, "I can do it myself." It demands a separated self to say it needs nothing else to survive. In reality, we need the universe, and in truth, it is ours for the taking if we let go of the results.

We must relax into the love of God that forms our very being, our source, our core, the substance of our lives, and our being.

This is who we are. This is our substance. This is what we can call for. This is the faith that Jesus called us into. This is ours for the asking. The faith of the mustard seed grows into a mighty tree.

We will look into each of these steps in more detail.

*"I have been driven many times upon my knees
By the overwhelming conviction that I had
nowhere else to go.
My own wisdom and that of all about me
Seemed insufficient for that day."*
—Abraham Lincoln

Questions to Ponder

If your life were running totally smoothly, you would not be reading these words. Think about the overall qualities of your life. Write down your feeling about the restless portion of your life.

Does it seem possible to move to the point of singing in your most inner being?

Write down your feelings about letting go of the results and breathing in the fragrance of the Holy Spirit.

Meditation

My Eternal Wisdom, my Guiding Light, the Creator, I bow to the inevitable presence that you bring into my life. I place myself at your center, the indwelling force that creates my spirit and the conscious awareness that life exists in and around and through me. I hold myself open to become aware of your spirit, to see that your love fills all that I see and am aware of. I lift my voice in gratitude for the certainty that life is eternal. I have a purpose beyond what I see, and joy and internal peace are my birthright. I acknowledge that I hold the keys to understand how to tap into that flow of energy. A life filled with abundance is waiting for me to grasp it. Give me the patience to accept the words of guidance that you offer me on this path.

Chapter 19

Step 1

When he saw the crowds,
He had compassion on them;
Because they were harassed and helpless,
Like sheep without a shepherd.
—Matthew 9:36, NIV

Step 1. We admitted we were powerless over our ego—that our lives were unmanageable and filled with unease and restlessness.

*P*ut your personal pain in this place. See yourself in this powerless point. *Admit it.* Do not let this go. This is *the* crucial point to moving to a faith beyond that of a mustard seed. Admission that you cannot do this alone is one of the most critical points required to achieve the faith that can move mountains. It is possible, but first we see that we, in our egoic state, cannot do this on our own. Up to now, we have usually only seen ourselves from the egoic center.

We have the power to change our lives and live a life of abundance—a life filled with joy and happiness. That process requires us to change our perceptions of the world we live in. Living a life of abundance or joy and happiness requires us to leap into the care of our Creator. This process cannot be accomplished within the context of our self-centered self—where we trust no one outside of ourselves—no matter how much we protest. All of us have been too battered by life and all the quirks therein to be able to have the level of trust in anything outside of what skills we can bring to the fore. Even those skills fail us at the most crucial moments, and things do not happen as we had hoped or wished.

Trust

The basic issue is that change is downright scary. We have lived in distrust for all of our lives, except when we were very small. Back then, most of us were in a protected cocoon. Everything we needed was provided—food, love, warmth, and protection from harm. As we grew older, we stepped outside that cocoon and found things that were not so comfortable. School forced us to challenge ourselves. We had to face others who were not so nice. Some

> *Have enough courage to trust love one more time and always one more time.*
> *—Maya Angelou*

were bullied. We had to learn how to be friends, compromise, and gain the knowledge that would allow us to become adults.

As adults, we had to learn to survive. If we were strong, we could move in ways that had others following us. We had to learn to fit in with others, for there were always others who were stronger than us. We had to develop skills to survive. We had to learn to get along. We had to learn to depend on others. If we were lucky, we could trust others to do their jobs so that we could do ours. The more we learned to do that—and some never have learned that and refuse to take a risk in anything—the wider the scope of things we can cover and grow.

Many of us learned to fit in, found jobs, housed ourselves, and fed our families. We soon began striving for outside events to bring us momentary joy, but we also grew in relationships. Most of them ended badly. If we were lucky, we learned how to grow gracefully in those relationships. If we were lucky, we found a compatible person and married. For many, even that move ended badly—once again seeming to prove that we can trust no one but ourselves.

No matter how things have turned out, we find holes in our lives that nothing seems to fill. Something was missing. The hole was still there. We started to fill that hole. Sometimes we found a drug—alcohol, sports, books, the Internet, television—and filled our lives with them so we did not have to think. When that was not enough, the emptiness in our lives became too much to bear. We started reading and searching, sometimes consciously and sometimes unconsciously.

The teacher will come.

You are not reading this by accident. A force greater than you put these words into your hands. The Eternal Force is always present, and when an opportunity presents itself in the form of a disaster, an accident, or a feeling, the Eternal Force presents alternatives. Eternal Wisdom is sneaky like that, giving us a nudge, a shove, a kick, or a battering ram to help us grow. When we are ready, God puts a teacher in place to give us tools to grow.

The teacher can be a book, a vision of bliss, a person we

> *When the student is ready*
> *The teacher will appear.*
> *—Anonymous*

meet, or a compatible soul who can read us like a book, but it is always a series of words and experiences that takes us to the next step in our journey.

I had a breathtaking visit in December 1967. Eternal Wisdom had made it clear that God would always be my guide and would never let me down. That left me dangling like a fish out of water. Shortly after that, a visionary came into a group I was in. She remained my mentor for three years, until we moved to upstate New York. She was a master, and introduced me to the teachings of Gurdjieff, a Russian mystic from the early 1900s. She had been a student of his. His writings, the writings of his followers, and the experiences of my mentor opened up possibilities that have never stopped expanding. They moved from possibilities to experiences to truths.

I gained a thirst for the sublime. I had to trust in this drive that lives within me to perceive more and more that all we have is an illusion—a glimpse similar to some of those 'stars' in our sky. When examined closely by powerful telescopes, they consist of millions or even billions of galaxies, each with billions of stars. What we see in our skies is an illusion of the truth, and what we see in our daily lives is an illusion of the truth of the miracles that exist in us and through us.

If we but see...

Just like the stars, the illusion of life can fool us into believing that there is nothing more to life than what we see.

And that is all we will see until we learn to trust the universe and all the great mysteries that spin out of nothing in each moment. Out of all the possible moments that could be, we have this moment, this 'now', in all its potential.

Each moment—each instant of time—is filled with possibilities.

If we but trust...

Trusting means abandoning what we think is truth—but is only an illusion for all the possibilities that could be.

To learn to trust, we admit that we have been powerless over how our lives have progressed to this point. The control we have over our lives is limited at best, and we have no cushion from the random events that come and go in our lives—no matter how great our lives seem on the outside. *"For I have the desire to do what is good, but I cannot carry it out"* (Romans 7:18, NIV).

In this first step, we admitted that we were powerless over the ego and that our lives were unmanageable and filled with unease and restlessness.

> *"The reason why many are still troubled,*
> *Still seeking, still making little forward progress*
> *Is because they haven't yet come to the end*
> *Of themselves. We're still trying to give orders,*
> *And interfering with God's work within us."*
> *—A.W. Tozer*

Step 1. We admitted we were powerless over our ego—that our lives were unmanageable and filled with unease and restlessness.

Questions to Ponder

How well do we trust ourselves? How well do we trust our families? How well do we trust our coworkers? How well do we trust our friends? How well do we trust our neighbors? How well do we trust the world?

Write down how your trust moves around the various layers of humanity: self, family, coworkers, friends, neighbors, and the world.

How do you believe Jesus, Buddha, Mother Teresa, or Nelson Mandela trusted the world? Write down your thoughts about these great humans and other great humans you can think about.

Meditation

Eternal Wisdom, you have taught me that all I see in our life is but an illusion to the truth that exists around and in me. I am striving to open my eyes and being to the possibilities that exist in your framework. Just as the skies above mask their truth, our lives mask the truth of your abiding presence. Help me see that all I hide behind in the ego prevents me from seeing the infinite possibilities that are there. I place my gratitude that you will keep the possibilities open to me for eternity, never giving up and knowing I will join you when I transition. I ask that you open me up to the possibilities that I may enter into the kingdom of God that dwells within me.

Chapter 20

Step 2

But while he was still a long way off,
His father saw him and was filled with
compassion for him;
He ran to his son, threw his arms around
him and kissed him.
—Luke 15:20, NIV

Step 2. We came to believe that a power greater than our egos could restore us to sanity.

*D*o you believe that a power greater than your egoic center can help you get to that point of seeing beyond the self? Can you admit that you cannot do it in your separated space? Only the power of God combined with your joining with that power and the recognition of our unity with God has the ability to change the apparent logical outcome. You and God are one, the Image of the Creator. We are individualizations of the Creator. Jesus said that the power was yours to take. What more do you want to hear? God told you that the power to change all is yours for the taking.

How can we be *"made in the image and likeness of God"* (Genesis 1:27, NIV)? Certainly not in any physical sense. God is the All in All, the Alpha and the Omega, the Beginning and the End. How are we made in God's image unless we are a part of the very being of the nature of God? If this is so, then we retain an infinite amount of power to do *"greater things than this"* (John 14:12, ESV).

Jesus said that even an "image of God" is infinite in its very nature since an image of infinity is infinity. Jesus told us that we are human and divine, that the indwelling of the Holy Spirit is our very soul, intrinsically bound to us as one. Saint Paul discussed the "Body of Christ" by saying that we are all part of the whole body— and just as a finger is not the whole body, but a part. Paul was speaking the truth given to him by God, which is the same truth that Jesus spoke.

Jesus wanted us to follow him—not worship him. We are to be imitators and followers of Jesus because we are *"co-heirs with Christ"* (Romans 8:17, NIV). We are not someone pulling on the strings of Jesus; we are "co-heirs." Jesus understood clearly who he was. We do not understand who we are.

That is our heritage. That is who we are. We can do, as Jesus said, *"greater things than this"* (John 14:12, NIV).

Greater things than this shall you do.

Jesus made this audacious statement, which has been watered down by almost all commentators since that time. Google that statement and look at all the mentions of the perceptions that Jesus was only stretching his argument, that in no way can we be equal to Jesus or do greater things than Jesus.

Part of me suspects I am a loser, And the other part of me thinks I'm God Almighty.
—John Lennon

But it is so bold a statement that it could not have been left out of the gospels since too many were aware of Jesus having said it. It is no wonder people wondered about the meaning of the statement.

The mystics present and past understood the truth of these statements. These statements clearly outlined what Jesus intended: we have the power to create miracles. When Jesus used the term *faith*, he meant that we had to move beyond the isolated self. Each of us has, in general, only one source of faith: ourselves and what we can do in the physical world.

This is so outrageous and so critical in our discussion that we need to review this point again. I added one more level to this discussion. If we are made in the "image of God," then the only possible way we could be in God's image is through our link with God. The inner soul is linked in some way to the very nature of God. Humans have distorted this message from Jesus ever since because the message was too good to be true. It did not fit the image of the Roman Empire when the New Testament books were approved in the fourth century. Can you imagine stating that everyone, including the 80 percent of the population that were slaves, were equal to God? That would have destroyed the empire. One cannot enslave God, and that concept had to go. Even if removing that concept destroyed the basic message Jesus came to give, it had to go!

The Wisdom of God

The message of Jesus is clear as recorded in the Bible, especially if we take the portions of the message of Jesus as most likely actually said by Jesus as studied by Bible scholars. We recognize that the earliest written words in the New Testament gospels were not written until about forty years after the death of Jesus; most followers of Jesus expected the immediate return of Jesus at that time; thus, no need to write the words down.

Only when his apostles began transitioning did they realize they should write things down. Only the most striking statements by Jesus in the gospel accounts can be considered actual words by Jesus. The Sermon on the Mount compiled many sayings of Jesus in a single spot, even though it is believed that these sayings actually occurred throughout the ministry of Jesus. They comprise the core messages of Jesus taught. Many so-called sayings of Jesus are there to emphasize the writer's point of view; the technique of using a famous person to mouth the author's worldview was a common approach to writing at that time. The tone of the words gives away the person who said the words.

The Wisdom of Science

Does science agree that we have the power to affect the outcome of our lives? As stated previously, science is in perfect agreement with all that I stated above. Quantum physics and all the experiments designed to prove or disprove the math have proven the strange outcomes predicted by quantum mechanics mathematics.

The most bizarre of the outcomes resulted in that there is only now; the past is but a memory, and the future is undetermined. That means that every sub-picosecond (one billionth of a second) and smaller moments of time (a trillionth of a trillionth of a trillionth of a second and smaller), there is a new now. The result has a possibility to be different than expected from the previous now since the very act of sensing that event (by our mind since the sensors of our bodies send the signals to our minds, which interpret our senses) modifies the event. This fact is in striking agreement with the Words of Jesus. *"Greater things than this shall you do,"* and *"You shall say to that mountain go throw yourself into the see, and if you have no doubt, it will happen"* (Mark 11:23, Combined several translations).

These statements talk about the future 'now' being totally different than the previous 'now'. The sayings of Jesus portray the essence of quantum physics.

Jesus said magic can happen, and he proved it with his miracles. Quantum physics says that magic can and does happen. Our very existence proves that. Small changes in the DNA of various forms, spurred by environmental events, brought life to be more life. These changes caused more life changes, first swimming, then crawling, to eventually become beings who can think and self-recognize. We call it evolution, and those of us who have dealt in genetic changes of plants by crossbreeding know that these events appear random, but they are guided by the genetic code and the environment.

When I helped my father hybridize garden lilies, we made certain crosses and hoped for an outcome. We harvested several dozen seeds from each crossing, planted them, waited a few years for them to bloom, and were amazed by the varying results. No two were the same. Subtle changes in the plant DNA meant subtle differences—and sometimes remarkable difference. There was only one cross, but there were so many differences since each seed was unique. If that year's cross did not achieve what was sought, we would try again the next year, hoping the results would be better.

Quantum physics goes beyond the randomness of possibilities and the potential for things other than the expected to occur. To the great surprise of the physicist—and the horror of those who claim there is no God—quantum physics enters into the world of the theologian. These findings are based upon the study of the smallest particles and astronomers and cosmologists who study the beginnings of the universe and the great mystery of the black holes. They study time itself and the very nature of the universe.

The Hadron Collider uses extreme pressure created by collision velocities to reveal the very nature of matter. Particles with strange names form all matter, both visible and not visible. That nature is shown to be identical to Einstein's general relativity equation, which showed the dual nature of matter and energy. That nature revealed by the equations and of the experiments is that nothing solid exists. No particle exists as a fundamental being, and all matter and energy are equal; in fact, only energy bonds exist.

All that exists is energy.

Energy is a force that cannot be created or destroyed. It forms relationships that bind with other relationships to create relativistic events that we call particles that bind together to form matter we can see and forces we can measure but not see. Atomic power uses the energy released when those relational bonds are broken.

We are fields of relationships.

All that exists is relationships that shift and slide to become all that we know. We can only get glimpses of their relationships in that small portion we can see, which is only about 0.01 percent of the measureable energy in our universe.

Is this a definition of God? Not all of God, but the portion we can grasp in our thoughts? Our universe has a beginning and an end, and it is within defined limits that we have calculated. We have the void outside of our universe. The study of black holes has begun to reveal some of that area, but we know there is no limit to what is outside our universe.

What else can we say that better defines God that we can understand? This is only in the four dimensions we can measure. Six or seven other dimensions exist by mathematical complexity. All of this is ours. We have the capacity because we are from the physical side of God, and we are part and parcel of God (see John 17).

But we have blinders on. These blinders form a purpose. They permit us to express ourselves with the unique branch of each of us. It is time to remove those blinders and see and understand who we really are.

We are part and parcel of God. We are not the full God of the universe and beyond. We are a tiny portion of God who contains the energy that is you and the energy that is me, and we contain the infinite capacity to fulfill our deepest desires once we merge with that universal truth, the ocean of God, with conscious effort.

I am not my body;
I am free.
I am as God created me.
—A Course in Miracles

Step 2. We came to believe that a power greater than our egos could restore us to sanity.

Questions to Ponder

Does the thought that a power greater than the egoic self can restore peace of mind, and bring joy and happiness seem real? Write down your musings on this question.

Does the thought that this power (the kingdom of God) that lies within (*"The Kingdom of God lies within"* – Luke 17:21, ESV) which can bring us eternal joy and happiness lies within our very being: all we have to do is tuck away our egos and enter into that "kingdom within." Does this seem possible?

Write down your thoughts in your journal.

Meditation

Eternal Wisdom, I am deeply grateful for living in an age when we have begun to have some understanding of the nature of God. You form all I am and are. You have given wisdom and foresight to this small portion of this universe, allowing me to experience all that makes up this moment of now. I am asking for the courage to become conscious of you, being always present and therefore with my true being, and to see the paradise I live in. Let my soul, that part of the Holy Spirit, loom ever larger in my recognition of what I am: God in an accessible, physical form, changing constantly, flowing from one another to another. I bow in wonder in this breathtaking venture I am on to reveal who I really am—that wonder of wonder, the image of God in this physical plane (see John 17:21-23).

Chapter 21

Step 3

*It is wonderful what miracles
God works in wills that are
Utterly surrendered to God.
—Hannah Whitall Smith*

Step 3. We made a decision to turn our will and our lives over to the care of God as we understood God.

*T*he hard part is surrendering ourselves into the power that surround us, fills us, and is our internal vital core. Let go and let God. The force that created our vast universe is ours for the taking. Do we dare? Can we turn our wills (our egos) over to that power and let that power become ours? The power of the Creator is ours for the asking. We let ourselves fall into that power and let go. Let God. Jesus called this "the faith of a mustard seed."

Turning Your Life Over

The key to living a life of abundance is to live in such a manner that you turn your life over to the care of our God. A question arises each day. Is this a day when we turn our lives over to the care of God—or do we strangle the power of God within us by choosing to live based on the drives of our egos? How does a person let go of all that grabs our attention and let the energy of God enliven us? Do we have to abandon our families, jobs, and all that forms our lives so we can live in contemplation and prayer?

Of course not. In fact, it is the opposite. When we surrender to God, the world takes on a whole new meaning. Our duties become a joy; even the most mundane tasks take on a life of their own and have meaning. And yes, it can bring in money, which is a good way to provide for our lives, giving us a place to call home, food, clothing, etc.

To be able to reach the infinite power of the universe means that we are in alignment with the universe so that the power can flow through us. When we are in the egoic center, we will be wherever our egos lead us, which is seldom in alignment with that of the universe. When we are in alignment with the universe, things flow much easier. The general path of our lives becomes easier and heads in a direction that eventually leads us to understanding we are living in abundance.

Living in Alignment with the Universe

Living a life that is in surrender to the care of God is identical to living a life in alignment with the universe. The universe is life itself. It is what we call God. This bold statement will return again and again. If God is the All in All, the Alpha and the Omega, then nothing is outside of God. If we— and the universe—are

We can only learn to know ourselves and do what we can—namely, surrender our will and fulfill God's will in us.
—Mother Teresa

not a portion of what we call God, then God is not the All in All (see Colossians 3: 1 and Corinthians 15:28), I have said this before, and I will say it many times in the future. This idea is called panentheism, or that God includes all the physical as well as all the non-physical aspects of all there is. This statement goes against what we have been told by our various religions, leaders, and wise persons in the past, except for Jesus: *"I pray that they will all be one, just as you and I are one – as you are in me, Father, and I am in you. And may they be one in us so that the world will believe that you have sent me."* John 17:21, NLT.

The God of my Understanding

What a strange way to express God. Is there only one God? Would God only be in one form? God is any form that there is. All forms are forms of God. If God is the All in All, then of course, all forms are forms of God. If I can say that God and the universe and life are one, look at the forms that exist in the universe. In all the forms that exist as humans, no two are alike. The God you understand is different than the God that is understood by every other human on the planet. Every perceptual process is different. We each carry a different perception of God in our hearts. We may say the same words, but each of us understands those words in a different manner.

God did not define herself in the form of Jesus as the only form possible, and saying that God is in the form of an adult male of any age is a form of insanity. Unfortunately, this form of insanity has been rampant on this planet to justify the male domination of society for five thousand years or more, based upon the histories engraved in the monuments of the world. Before that time, statues seem to indicate that objects of worship were more feminine, often pregnant or exaggerated female forms, but that is another story.

The God of our understanding has changed with the culture—and within the culture of each individual. It changes many times for each person. The God I understand today is only a little like the God of my understanding of even a few years ago.

I am sure the God of my understanding of today will continue to change throughout my life—and will change even more in the next phase of my life after my limited physical being is freed into the internal realm.

So it is in the care of the God of my understanding; in the form of the universe, (God is the All in All, including the physical universe) that enables the forces of the universe to align with our needs and gives us a life of abundance, that form of life that brings us joy and peace of heart.

How often do I turn the day over to God?

Each day is the beginning of a new turn and phase of your life. The phrase, which may seem trite, *"Today is the first day of the rest of your life,"* is true. When you wake in the morning, the world is beginning anew, fresh with promise, with the potential of all kinds of promising potential. Fresh in the morning is the best time to spend even a few seconds being grateful for the new day, no matter what you have on the schedule for the day. Just to be alive for one more day is a gift of life, even if that day is your last day in this cycle of life. Each day is a blessing, a time to share with your God a gift of the one thing that is always present: your now. This instant of awareness marks you as a conscious being, capable of the most precious thing in the universe: a time to commune, even if for a moment, and even if you feel nothing in return, to commune with your God.

The Gift of Now

There is only now. There is no past. It is gone and will never be repeated in this lifetime. There is no future since that depends on the choices we make at each moment. We create our own futures by what we do and believe in this now. Each now comes and comes and comes. A small change in perspective will change the next now, which will lead to the next change in the following now. Soon we have a totally different outcome than if had made a different choice way back in that first now when we first perceived a possible change. A life of abundance occurs one now at a time.

Are we willing to step into the future? It is a big change in behavior, and change is always scary—if not downright frightening. We have settled into our behavior patterns by default, thinking that is all there is. It is not so. We are free to change our ways of thinking at any time. Nothing prevents us from seeing things differently, in a fresh light—perhaps lit from within—glowing in the light of God.

The world we see is an illusion.

We see the world according to the perspective we bring to the world. If we change that perspective, we change the world we see. It is that simple. Do we see the glass of the world as half-full or half-empty? It is only a matter of perspective. If we want a life of abundance, we will see the world in one way. If let the ego take control, we will see the world in a totally different way. The first will see the world as inherently good, expecting good things to happen and seeing good things happen. The latter will see the world as hostile to them, expecting the worst and seeing the worst as it appears to happen.

There is only the now, this very instant. I will be repeating this many times. It is a difficult concept to grasp and accept in one's own life. We normally see the past, with all its impacts on our lives, and we live out much of our lives trying to change the past, grieving for the past, and wishing the past to be different. We often fail to see what is happening right now.

We can live in a dream about the future, imagining all kinds of scenarios that could happen. We might fail to see what is happening right in this instant. Now is the only time there is. None of that potential glorious future will occur unless we do something now to make the shift toward what could occur in the future.

Living in the past and the future fails to look at the now (the only time there is). Watching the now and moving it in a direction that will fill more positive possibilities will make the future unfold in abundance.

The Power of Now

God only has one moment, and that is 'now'. All time is an illusion in this level of consciousness. God sees the eternal, all moments in time (what I call the no-time), and is aware of all the potential of the choices we could make (or don't make) and the potential outcomes of all these choices. We make our choices, and that destiny unfolds before us—moment by moment, choice by choice, 'now' by 'now'. We can make the decision to place our lives in the hands of the Eternal Wisdom and rest assured that the All in All will only give us the very best so that we may become the person we were created to become.

We turn our lives over for God. God will be the guide for a life of abundance.

> *Surrender your own poverty and acknowledge your nothingness to God. Whether you understand it or not, God loves you, dwells in you, calls you, saves you and offers you an understanding and compassion which are like nothing you have ever found in a book or heard in a sermon.*
> *—Thomas Merton*

Step 3. We made a decision to turn our wills and our lives over to the care of God as we understood God.

Questions to Ponder

Can you see yourself turning your life over to the care of God (your higher power) as you understand God at this moment? Can you turn over everything in your past, everything in your future, and right where you are this moment?

Write down your internal feelings about the process of letting God (your higher power) operate your life.

The kingdom of God lies within you. Heaven is waiting within your grasp. Can you accept the arms of God to enfold you in joy?

Write down how that feels in your heart.

Meditation

My Eternal Life Force, who has shown me eternal love and care, I acknowledge in gratitude your desire to show me only love and support. I know that our limited ability in this form of experience too often prevents me from seeing the abundance, the joy and happiness, in the step ahead if I but choose you and not my ego. I too often am afraid to trust myself to your care, despite the many times you have told me to trust you, as the birds of the air trust in your goodness to provide them all they need. I offer myself in faith to your care, putting my trust in your love and willingness to guide me to fulfill my purpose, to taste paradise on earth, and live out the return of Jesus on earth in one another.

My beloved Creator, I give myself over to your care, knowing deep in my heart that you will never permit something destructive to my soul to occur. I place all my trust in your loving goodness, give my future over to your care, and let go of my anxieties about the future and the guilt over the past. All will be well, and I can rest in that wonderful knowledge until we meet in the future.

Chapter 22

Step 4

Then you will know the truth
And the truth will set you free.
—John 8:32, NIV

Step 4. We made a fearless examination of what was preventing us from surrendering our lives over to the care of God as we understood God.

This step is one of the keys to living a life of abundance and finding lasting joy, happiness, and peace of mind. We have discussed how a true life of abundance requires us to commit to steps that seem to be the opposite of what the great American alliance states: self-reliance. How can we have self-reliance and surrender ourselves over to the care of our God? Why can't we find peace, joy, and happiness within us where we are? What is preventing us?

We have left ourselves drifting on the whims of fate, of every idea and concept that comes along, neither seeing nor sensing the infinite power granted us by God who "made us in the image and likeness of God" (Genesis 1). Only by aligning ourselves with the universe, which is the creative power of our God, can we discover who we really are. It is through the universe that all creation stems, and the universe is God in the form of energy (whatever that is). The primitive creative force is part of what we have called God, for God is Life.

We are creative, and so are all images of God. We have not been aware of the creative power we hold as part of our basic natures. The process of aligning ourselves with the universe gives us access to this infinite creative power. By letting ourselves flow with the quest of our souls in this life, the result will be joy, happiness, and peace of mind—no matter what occurs from the viewpoint of the world, including what occurs as we transition from this physical reality.

We all have fears of letting go of our lives, especially of letting ourselves immerse into the realm where we cannot worry. We can't be afraid of what could happen and let ourselves float in the results of what occurs— even though we had a different result in mind. Note that I said different and not better or worse. The result will be the best it can be, given the purpose we came into this life to find.

This fourth step is the step where we take the time to look deeply into our own inner drives. We should write down the parts of our lives that we are afraid to look at: fears, worries, concerns, anger, grievances, and anxieties. Those parts of our lives constrain us and limit our thinking.

The Journal

This is a key portion of our journey into a life of joy and happiness. We are to keep a record of where we are, especially in those areas where we feel hindered in our growth to a life of peace, joy, and happiness. We can see the progress that occurs every day, month, and year. This record provides us insights into the journey, gives us insights into where we have been, and points out the ever-changing path we are on each day.

Your journal does not have to be elaborate. It could as simple as a notepad, a yellow pad, or an electronic record. I have used all forms in the past. I presently use the program My Writing Spot and make sure I keep a backup version in the world of the cloud. This is critical. I lost much of my journal when I changed computers. The stored events did not pass into the new computer and were lost. This included many conference notes, book notes, and my personal journal.

I record my daily meditation practice and any thoughts that come into my head when I am putting data in. I try to keep it all separate by using separate journal titles. The electronic version allows me to move from one topic to another, keeps all in a single place, and allows me to view and write in many different topics rapidly. It transfers between my computer and my iPad with the touch of a button.

The journal becomes a road map of our story. This is important when we become discouraged in our journeys. When things look bleak, we cannot see the wonderful outcomes that will come because we are buried in the weeds. If we look at our journals during those times, we will see how far we have come. In each of the seemingly low periods in our lives, amazing things have happened to bring abundance and happiness into our lives.

Depending on your memory, the journal may only need brief descriptions and concepts to trigger the memories of actual events. Usually it requires a more detailed account to trigger the long term memory. When years have passed, and the memory is vague, it can take an even more detailed account. Don't stint in the account. It does not have to be every day, but it should be whenever something brings a critical turning point to mind, usually in hindsight and often months after the event.

What are we looking for in this process?

- shame and guilt
- fears
- worries
- anger
- concerns
- resentments
- pride

Shame and Guilt

All of us have done things we are ashamed of doing. Sometimes we carry this guilt and shame around for decades—and often for all of our lives. We bury it under piles of things that are called fun: alcohol, recreational drugs, endless TV, sporting events, or spiritual practices to cover shame and guilt.

We can rationalize what we did, but we cannot forgive ourselves and let it go. We fail to see that we did the best that we could do in those moments. In hindsight, it could have been better, but that was the best we could do then. We demand that we be perfect. We judge ourselves as inadequate and flog ourselves mentally. We all have these events in our lives, but we need someone who will listen, acknowledge the event, and help us point out all we have done to move past that event—even if it was a repeated event for many years.

Shame and guilt are the most debilitating forms of negativity that we can bear, and they spread into all parts of our lives. I speak from personal experience, having a "burden to bear," as Saint Paul puts it. I spent years living a part of my life in shame and guilt. I was not able to move away from the overwhelming sense of shame and guilt

All my life I feared imprisonment, the nun's cell, the hospital bed, the places where one faced oneself without distraction, without the crutches of other people.
—Edna O'Brien

until I used the twelve steps of Alcohol Anonymous. I eventually forgave myself and uncovered the low level of depression that is part of my nature. I accepted it as part of my shadow.

These steps to a life of abundance are modeled after the AA twelve steps, and they were a gift from God for a particular problem. A wonderful behavior-modification therapist taught me how to spare myself aggravating times that can spark the depression and use tools to bring joy into my life. These include joyful music (I am listening to Dixieland right now), keeping myself away from unnecessary tension by avoiding most movies and television, and not watching the news.

We will talk about dealing with our dark side—Carl Jung called it the *shadow*—in another chapter. God has put therapists into our lives to help pave the way for peace and joy.

Fear

The next group of negative events concerns the fears that fill us with apprehension, worry, and anger. Fear is the opposite of love, and only love can overcome the basic fears that fill our lives. For, as strange as it may seem, even fear is a form of love. It may be distorted, but it still is a form of love. If we did not love something, why would we have fears? Fear is the result of the potential of losing something that we love.

Love is a continuum that extends from the highest form—divine love—all the way to hatred. That is an extreme form of debilitating fear. It has been pointed out many times that love is the only true emotion in the universe. Love can be expressed in healthy ways (a mother for her child) and destructive ways (killing). Paralyzing fears can be catatonic.

Most of our fears are the result of personal events, and they often prevent us from fulfilling our potential in life. Fear of being mugged in a large city prevents us from enjoying the wonders of the city. Fear of potential terrorism prevents us from participating in life and makes us hate particular religious or ethnic groups. Fear of speaking in public prevents us from expressing who we are. It is best to put these down in your journal. They are a critical part of your life, and you must be willing to put these fears into the hands of God to better align yourself with the creative forces of the universe.

Worries

Worries are about the things that may happen, but in truth, they seldom occur. Jesus said, *"Do not worry about your life, what you will eat or drink, what you will wear. Is not life more than food, and the body more than clothes? Look at the birds of the air that do not sow, nor reap, nor gather into barns, and yet your heavenly Father feeds them. Are not you worth much more than they?"* (Matt. 6:25, NIV).

Worries form a wall that sometimes suffocates us, preventing us from living with joy and happiness. In fact, any worry, no matter how small, prevents us from the level of joy and happiness that God is offering us at all times. Worries are invisible, nagging feelings. Should I be doing something about that? Will I have the money for the mortgage or the rent? Will I be able to buy food? Can I get the car repaired?

A worry will never solve the problem. It won't pay the rent, it won't reduce the ice on the road, and it won't do anything to alleviate any concerns. All worry does is debilitate the ability to do something to help. Ask for advice if you can, turn it over to the care of God, and expect that all will turn out for the best.

I speak from much experience. When I was laid off from my job in 1970, child number five was a year old. I gave the results over to my God, concentrated on my new job of finding a paying job, my wife took a job selling menswear at Gimbal's Department Store, and we cut expenses all that we could. I asked the bank for several months off from paying the mortgage, which they gave. I was only out of work for two months, mainly because we were willing to move. The others who were laid off with me who I kept track of refused to consider that option. My wife and I left it all up to God after doing our best, and God responded by showing us a better way to live and raise children in the foothills of the Adirondack Mountains.

I could tell many more similar stories, especially from owning a small business during the last financial downturn.

Anger

How many times have we held anger over events? It can last for years or a lifetime, severing families and friendships. What so-and-so did was unforgiveable. How can I possibly let it go? The primary damage anger gives is to ourselves. Many times, the person we are so angry with has no idea why we are angry with them. They sometimes don't even know (or care) that we are angry.

I could not drop my anger at someone who had said some very nasty things about my wife in my presence. It was years before I could put it aside even though my wife ignored it completely and moved on. I cannot tell you how often I tried, but it was a fixture in my life for more than a decade. By using the twelve-step program, I was able to accept the event and move on.

Concerns

Concerns are a lesser evil than fears, even though they are a minor form of fear. We are concerned that our children or grandchildren may not measure up to some mark we may have decided. We are concerned that our favorite team will not win. We are concerned that our car may break down. These are the same as fears and worries, but of a lesser nature. They must eventually go if we are to have peace of mind, joy, and happiness.

Resentments

Most of us love resentments. We savor our resentments carefully, guard them well, and never let them go. They often seem to define us. So-and-so has a better house than me and is not as smart as me.

Resentments flare up often as a part of anger, and they form blocks to the path to peace of mind, joy, and happiness that are difficult to remove. Resentments are usually the other person's fault. People say, "I have the right to feel resentful for what they are." Unfortunately, the other person usually hasn't a clue that you are resentful of them. All that energy is lost in your own personal paranoia. We can resent life for not making us smarter, more attractive, or richer. Resentments are the killers of joy. They eat us up over things we have no control over. They effectively block us from joy and happiness.

These resentments must be written down and acknowledged.

Pride

Pride is a combination of fear, resentment, and self-aggrandizement that leaves us in pain and confusion, usually masked behind resentments and anger. Pride is important to one's life. Pride is usually thinking of one's self beyond what is reality and acting more important than one is. Pride

We are all serving a life sentence in the dungeons of the self.
—Cyril Connolly

has a side to it that is seldom recognized: being humble. Refusing to accept another's thanks often give rise to behavior patterns that present one's self in manners that are not reality. Pride is the chief adornment of the ego and prevents us from acknowledging that a better way awaits us if we give them away.

These sides of ourselves are recognized in our journals as we discover them. They are blocks to greater joy and happiness. These entry items are only a part of what we need to acknowledge in our lives. As we uncover them, they lift burdens from our minds, remove barriers to true freedom, and give us more room to align our lives with our souls. They permit us to live in joy and happiness in a life of abundance. This is not a one-time event. The path we are on will be revisited time and again if we are to maintain our internal peace and joy.

The free person is one who is not weighed down by negative emotions. He or she accepts our shadows when they appear, corrects the action, and moves on, putting all these events of our past in the proper place (in the past). Only then can we be free to accept with gratitude the freedom that comes with living in our souls' desires.

Neale Donald Walsch said, *"Life is the greatest gift. It exists as an opportunity for you to create and recreate yourself anew in each golden moment of now in the next grandest version of the next grandest vision you ever held about Who You Are."*

This is the purpose of life. This is why we are here in this life of physicality. This is the purpose of the twelve steps we are taking.

> **Darkness cannot drive out darkness:**
> **Only light can do that.**
> **Hate cannot drive out hate:**
> **Only love can do that.**
> **—Martin Luther King Jr.**

Step 4. We made a fearless examination of what was preventing us from surrendering our lives to the care of God as we understood God.

Questions to Ponder

Where are your blind spots in your life? Where are your fears, resentments, all those things that pull you down into the shadow? Write them down into your journal to see.

Meditation

Our Eternal Wisdom, I bow in gratitude for this opportunity to lose these weights that have burdened my life. Once expressing these burdens, I can place them into the proper place in my life—in the past. I accept gratefully the relief I gain in this process, made to move on with my life to a place of inner peace. I acknowledge my humanness, and I am beginning to understand that I am perfect in your eyes, acting as you created me to act, and moving forward to where I can express the next highest version of your vision for my life. I am grateful for the shadows you have granted me because they keep me grounded and acknowledging that you are the joy of my life. By surrendering all to you, I will find perfect freedom, joy, and happiness.

Chapter 23

Step 5

Repentance is the renewal of life.
—Thaddeus of Vitovnica

Step 5. We admitted to God, to ourselves, and to another person the nature of our fears, resentments, worries, anxieties, and grievances.

This is the step where we lay it all out in the open. We want to change. We want to find peace of mind, joy, and happiness. We want to live a life of abundance, but do I want to talk about it? No way! Unfortunately, that is not how life functions. Saying that, I can add that it is sometimes not necessary to talk to someone, and there are times it is advisable not to talk to someone.

I know people who have successfully not talked to someone in step 5, but it is highly recommended. You can try to make it fine without talking to someone, but life will remain the same. You will remember how you were supposed to talk to someone. You will procrastinate more, and your life will continue to shuffle out of control until you decide to give it a try.

When you finally decide to try, this input will be very useful to you. In the meantime, read this and store it for future reference—and then read it again. This process is critical.

Please give it a try. No step can be eliminated. There are some parts of your life that may be best not to reveal, but those occasions are rare. Plan on talking out all your shortcomings to a good listener.

Catholics have an advantage in this step. The Sacrament of Reconciliation serves much of the same purpose. We study ourselves, tell the priest what we consider we have done wrong, and we are forgiven in the name of God.

The fifth step has a similar form. We talk about our wrongs and our general outlook on life, including fears, worries, and concerns. The aspects of our lives that cause us shame and guilt are called "defects of character" in twelve-step circles. We do not deal with things that have no impact on our state of being. We put our lives out on the line, especially those portions of our lives that are preventing us from giving ourselves into the care of God.

The One Who Listens

When choosing a person to listen to your story, choose someone you trust with your personal story. Choose someone who will not share it with anyone without your permission and who will listen carefully. Choose someone who will ask questions to understand the event sufficiently to acknowledge what occurred and move on to the next event. A good suggestion is your best friend so you will be at ease with one another. Tell that person beforehand what you expect from this moment in your life. Explain how you are releasing the burdens that have weighed you down and prevented you from evolving. This cleansing moment is an acknowledgement of your unwanted past, which needs to be left behind in order to evolve. You are not asking for advice; you are stating that so-and-so occurred and is weighing you down.

The principle key to choosing the person is that person's ability to be discrete and accept what you are saying. This is why a professional therapist understands all and is bound by a code of ethics from telling anyone about a client. A priest and/or minister are also trained in this manner. Anyone who has been active in a twelve-step program like Alcohol Anonymous and is a sponsor in that program is a good candidate since this step is a key step in AA's twelve-step program.

A good friend will never reveal anything to imply what you will have said to them. You must have absolute confidence in the person.

After years have passed, it might not be necessary to talk about it. As the level of problems diminishes,

When we are listened to, it creates us, it makes us unfold and expand.
—Karl Menninger

you will be the recipient of these discussions with someone else.

The Event of Cleansing

Choose a quiet time when you will be interrupted and set the stage for a true celebration. Use whatever is comfortable for you, but a beer, a glass of wine, or anything you would use in a celebration would not be amiss.

Be sure to describe what you expect from your chosen person. The main part is to listen and acknowledge your description of the event or feeling. Your remaining feelings form a barrier. Details beyond what you describe are not necessary and are to be added only if your perspective is not clear to the listener.

Most of us do not have anything serious—from a legal viewpoint—that needs to be guarded from revelation. Most of what we need to say will say will be seen as benign and silly to be such a blocking point in our lives, but these events have formed giant blocks in our mind. They need to be laid to rest if we are to evolve. Your chosen listener is not to downplay any of your feelings. These feelings, demons, or defects of character are yours, and they are real to you.

Acknowledging Your Life

We have lived our lives in what most believe to be in a reasonable manner. We have made mistakes. We could have been more tolerant. We could have treated some folks nicer. Our fears have sometimes driven us to act in unreasonable ways, but in general, we think our lives have not been too bad.

We feel restless. We know that happiness is there for some folks, but something is missing for us. We may have tried different programs, attended lectures, or read self-help books, but something is missing.

We are missing a cleansing in our lives—an acknowledgement of who and what has formed our lives. We are missing a sense of who we are at this point in our lives. Our lives have been grand adventures, but it is time to put our past into the past. It will reside in peace, and we can live in the now. The present is all there is in the eyes of God. God does not consider anything we have done in the past to be a mistake or a sin, but certain events have failed to bring us to the next level of being. At the very least, they are preventing us from moving into the promised life of joy and happiness.

This cleansing process is a mark of moving on in our maturity and evolutionary process. This event needs to be savored for its healing capability. It should be celebrated. Sharing a beer, a glass of wine, a soft drink, or a water—or whatever makes you feel most comfortable as a means of celebration—is a good way to do this step. It marks the moment when we leave the past behind. Those events have caused pain over the years. This release permits us to have the space to welcome paradise and discover the peace and joy of God. It brings a world of happiness into our lives and transcends the outer world we live in.

Putting It All on the Line

This is who we are. Some of the events will seem almost silly. A childhood squabble that has forever changed a relationship. Sometimes we will not be able to remember what the disagreement was about, but it may have spoiled a relationship and needs to be put to bed. Sometimes it will be with someone who has passed on before you had an opportunity to discuss it. Sometimes it will be very serious—perhaps a spouse cheated or was a bully or someone bullied us in school.

When I was in high school, being bullied proved to be a large barrier to my growth, and it took some talking to work that out of my system and forgive them. When I returned for a high school reunion many years later, no one remembered any of the events that were such a sore point in my life. They all remembered a much more positive point in life than I did. I had built up such a barrier to my growth from the events, and no one else, including those in my mind that had created such events, could remember any negative interactions. I recalled only the negative parts and did not recall many of the joys of that time. What a waste of my time spent bemoaning and resenting those years when I could have rejoiced in the positive times instead.

It needs to be put into the past. Acknowledge the event or feeling, give it over to the care of God, and go to the next one. This process cannot be hurried; take one step at a time. Use all the time necessary. It may take more than one meeting, but the process is the important part. It all must be included, except legal items that are between you and God.

> *Maturity is when you are able to say,*
> *"It's not just them. It's me."*
> *—Criss Jami*

Step 5. We admitted to God, ourselves, and another person the nature of our fears, resentments, worries, anxieties, and grievances.

Questions to Ponder

Telling your story removes a load you did not realize you had, and the surprising feeling of relief can make you almost giddy. Write down how you felt after the session.

The release of the past is an important step in claiming a new future. The tentacles of the past are very strong, and they are reluctant to be removed from their hold on your being.

Write down how releasing these past events creates a new path for your being at this point and how you feel about this moment in time.

Meditation

My Beloved Wisdom, you have shown me the path of growth. I humbly open myself, making myself (at least in my own mind) vulnerable to others, but making it possible to remove the burdens that have made my life uncomfortable. These burdens have prevented me from finding the paradise you have offered me, but it is there for my claim. I acknowledge in gratitude this opportunity to reclaim my birthright and know once again who I am so I can move more deeply into the mystery of the universe.

I am open to the release of the past at this moment in time, and I let myself rest in your care during this time of cleansing. I am open to receive your blessings, and I am grateful for the opportunity to place things in perspective in my life—healing and rejuvenating my life in all.

Chapter 24

Step 6

Surrender is a choice; it is never a calling.
—Craig D. Lounsbrough

Step 6. We ask God to remove these barriers to a full and rich life—one filled with joy and happiness.

*T*his is the step of surrender, and we let all these issues in our lives flow over to the care of God. Now is the moment to let go of all and let God handle all the sorrows we are carrying in our lives. It is a relief to let these burdens be handled by the Creator of the universe. God can create anew the life we are living and move us into alignment with the energy flows of the universe so we can move into the level of creative power that is ours to claim.

It will be surprisingly difficult to surrender our burdens. We have become very attuned to these burdens of ours, and we suddenly find ourselves clinging to them. We are afraid to let them go. We are afraid that we will lose a vital part of our being. These burdens are ours, and nobody had better fool with them. We hesitate, wait, and procrastinate, wondering what we are losing.

This is the ego speaking. It is the self-centered part of our being that we have carefully built up over all our lives into a formidable barrier that isolates us from perceived blows that come from outside ourselves. Our egos are trying to survive. They know that if we give all our burdens away, they will have no place to cling to. They will gradually wither, and our souls will come forth and direct our lives in a manner that befits a creator of the universe, but above all will benefit ourselves by reducing the self-inflating ego.

Ego

The ego is an important part of our lives. It is the side of our lives we need to do the ordinary functions of our lives. The ego performs all the functions we need to live, work, and operate as a citizen of the world. Balancing between the id (instinctual drives, such as eating, fear, and reproduction) and the superego (the part of our training that understands the strictures of society and religion), the ego provides structure to our lives for everyday events. Over time, it builds structure in our lives and forms all the central meaningful events (good and bad). The ego defines who we are to ourselves, acknowledges the structures around us, sets our limits of actions, and effectively runs our lives.

The ego forms a central part of our lives—neither good nor bad—and allows us to function in life. This is good, as far as it goes. Eventually though, the ego becomes another person in our lives. Its thoughts appear to be separate from us and what we should be doing. It begins to dictate the way we act and our responses. It takes our experiences and turns them into weapons to strengthen its own functionality. It batters us into doing its bidding. The functions of the ego become our driving functions, and they control all that we do—until we have had enough and look outside the ego for something better.

That is the purpose of these twelve steps. They are a guide to freedom. They free us from the drives of the ego. They free us from the instinctual drives of the id and the controlling drives of the superego. You may have felt that there must be more joy and more happiness.

Sigmund Freud could see these three forces in the conscious mind, but the conscious mind has many other forces. C. J. Jung added another component that he called the Shadow. The shadow includes the parts of our consciousness that reflect our negative drives. The soul is the part that reflects the positive drives. He wrote a differing viewpoint from Freud of the human psyche that included the spiritual side of the psyche (the soul) that provided for a profound influence on the person. These discussions and variations in the early twentieth century led to a strong sentiment in a group known as the Oxford Group (known later as

Moral Rearmament). They influenced an alcoholic, Bill Wilson, who had a strong conversion experience. As a result, he formed what is now known as Alcoholics Anonymous and wrote the twelve steps. These twelve steps of abundance I have put forth in this book are a development of the original 12 steps of Alcoholic Anonymous. Bill, as he was known throughout AA, communicated with Jung, who greatly appreciated and approved of the original twelve steps and what they said.

When I speak of the ego, I am also including the framework established by Jung. We are too complex to be thought of only as id, ego, and superego. We are learning to move around these complexities (id, ego, superego, and the shadow) and put them in their proper places in our lives.

In this terminology, the ego is the portion of consciousness that supports our goals. If properly used, it forms us into a productive being in society. In almost all of us, the ego becomes a leading force that dominates our thinking and being. This leads to isolation from the soul, the portion that recognizes our oneness of being with all that is. The ego creates individualism that prevents us from evolving into the God-beings we were meant to become. When the ego becomes dominant, it creates angst that leaves us with a bewildering amount of unease and dissatisfaction. It can drive us to seek satisfaction in life by means that form distractions rather than satisfaction.

This is the time that symbols and signs appear in our lives. If we are the least bit awake, we will follow them to see where they go.

These twelve steps were formed in my life to give me the perspective I am sharing in this treatise. You would not be reading this if your inner forces were not guiding you to seek a wider vision and purpose in life.

Letting Go

Letting go of the ego and surrendering the portion of our being that has formed our central awareness of who we are is a difficult step. Generally we give it up only to take it back, again and again. This process continues throughout life for most of us. We have

> *The ego hates losing—even to God.*
> *—Richard Rohr*

spent all or most of our lives building up and relying on our egos. They do not want to surrender and reduce their holds on us. One day we give it to God, intending to surrender, but the next day, the ego takes control of our lives again and we take it all back – including the pain.

How important is this step? Marianne Williamson, one of the guiding lights of *A Course In Miracles* and a member of AA, states:

> *"At a certain point, it doesn't really matter so much how we got to be a certain way. Until we admit our character*

> *defects—and take responsibility for the fact that regardless of where we got them, they are ours now—God has no power to heal them. We can talk to a therapist for hours about how our relationship with Mom or Dad made us develop a certain behavior characteristic, but that of itself will not make it go away. Naming it, surrendering it to God, and asking God to remove it—that's the miracle of personal transformation. It won't go away in a moment, necessarily, but its days are numbered. The medicine is in your psychic bloodstream." (Day 5, A Year of Miracles)*

This step is not to be taken lightly. It is the key to transforming your life from a life catering to the ego and all its whims to a life of abundance. All of life can be a source of joy—even heart-wrenching moments or life-changing events. You can find joy hidden behind sorrow, physical pain, and gut-wrenching occurrences.

Some key points in the quote from Marianne need to be expanded upon.

God has no power to heal them.

This statement may shock you, but God will not—and cannot—violate your free will. As long as you cling to these demons and call them your own, they will remain. One of the few things that God has placed limits on God's own power is not violating your free will. Your will is God's will.

God knows that you will eventually release these demons, and since God lives in the eternal now—where all time and possibilities are now—God knows that you will someday see the light of day. Your will, which is as strong as God's will—and in this case *is* God's will—will give up these demons. Your will is God's will made manifest. You are the living extension of God, the experiential part of God that can experience God's own joy and love through you. That is why a life of abundance is possible. If you do not like your life, you can choose a different life, but you choose that life. That manner of choosing is what these twelve steps are all about.

Naming the Character Defect

In step 4, we wrote down all the negative feelings and emotions that dragged us down. This is the process of naming the demons that hound us. These are the areas of life—actions, fears, resentments, and anger—that prevent us from soaring like eagles. These are the demons that bound us as surely as the fiercest rope. We cannot release them via our own actions. These character defects include actions we cannot forgive ourselves. We have decided that those actions are too terrible for even God to forgive, and we hang on to them, often defining ourselves by them.

We have to name them, see them for what they are in our lives, accept them as part of ourselves, lay them down in the arms of our God, and let God absorb them and wash them away in the ever flowing river of the grace of God. Each act we name limits what the ego can hold onto and beat us over the head with.

They are ours.

These character traits that we abhor are ours, and we have guarded them jealously. They have formed a part of our personality—whether we have admitted them before or not. Without these parts of our lives, we feel almost naked. Only by losing our character defects will our real selves begin to shine. All these negative parts need be erased from our psyches, and by laying them in the arms of God, we begin the process of healing. In step 5, we stated them to another person, clearly owned them, and stated our desire to eliminate them from our lives.

Surrender to God.

We must be willing to part with the areas of our lives that have formed such big parts of our personalities. The act of surrender is frightening, but it promises us that we will be free! What a strange, compelling, frightening world awaits us. We are free to be who we really are. Can we live with ourselves when that happens?

We take several deep breaths, and we ask God to remove all the problem areas and our demons. And God will, when asked.

At this point, a great sense of relief may occur. The worst things have been laid out on the table and given to God. This action assures us that God will remove them. The timing of the removal is not up to us, but it does depend on the depth of our commitment to remove them.

Marianne Williamson states that we may see them crop up in the future, but their intensity will gradually diminish and their days are numbered. We have been inoculated with the saving grace of this step and God's promise. If we continue on this path where we draw deeper into the wellspring of God's love, our Eternal Wisdom will fill us more and more as time flows by.

This is the miracle of personal transformation.

The journey is what brings us happiness.
Not the destination.
—Dan Millman

Step 6. We ask God to remove these barriers to a full and rich life—one filled with joy and happiness.

Questions to Ponder

Does asking God to remove these burdens fill you with joy or trepidation? Write down your feelings about this process.

Does the thought that you are about to lose a portion of your personality frighten you? Write down your feelings.

Meditation

My Eternal Wisdom, once again, I bow in gratitude for this opportunity to evolve to my next highest version of the highest vision I have ever had of myself. There are no words to express my inner joy and the relief I feel by casting off all these demons that have haunted me through the years. I am willing to follow you as you lead me onward into a life of abundance. I am amazed by how you show me—at the time I am wondering what is next—the next step in my evolution. I hold my breath for the future, knowing that all is ready for me for the rest of my life to live in your love forever. I know you will never abandon me, and I depend on your guidance for this life into the next. I will depend on you to follow my efforts and guide them along the higher path that will bring me joy and happiness—now and in the future.

Chapter 25

Step 7

God is love,
And they who abide in love,
Abide in God.
—1 John 4:16, ESV

Step 7. We acknowledge both the light and dark elements of our nature as to who we are in the deeper reality of our being.

*H*uman nature contains light elements and dark elements. God created this apparent duality within us as part of the evolutionary beings we are. Without the dark side (or shadow side), we would have nothing to evolve from or to since we would already be perfect in form and nature.

The shadow is not a mistake by God; it is part of the perfection of who we are in this created form. By accepting and welcoming our seemingly dual nature—and treating it as it is as a gift from the Eternal

Wisdom—we begin to understand the wisdom of our universe.

Our Creator has given us the greatest gift. We are creatures of free choice and can choose the path to the highest evolution quickly or slowly. We cannot miss the goal of perfection. We are perfect in our essence since we are wavelets of God, or as it says in Genesis 1, "made in the image of God". The tip of a wave is part of the ocean, but it is not *all* of the ocean. We are a part of what we term God, but we are not all of God (see John 17:21).

Jung called it an "individualization" of what we know as God. God is so much greater than what we can understand, and the reality is beyond comprehension. We have been given glimpses of the divine, and I breathed some of that pure essence many years ago. An amazing number of people have had breathtaking experiences with the essence we call God.

The Image of God

Humanity is made in the *"image and likeness of God"* (Genesis 1). We contain the essence of that portion of God that is always learning and changing. Surprise: God is always learning and changing, and we, the image of God, relish that process in the center of our being – even when we are afraid of that process.

One of the greatest joys of humanity is learning something new and changing how one thinks of the universe. One of the wonders of the world is the constant gaining of knowledge of the universe and all it consists of. We are made in the image of God. Since curiosity and a thirst for knowledge and experience are parts of the created essence of humanity, we find great joy in gaining knowledge and experience. Will we not bring that knowledge and experience back into the essence of our Creator when we join with God after passing from this creation? Is this mission of discovery and experience the essence of what we can ·perceive of what we call God?

This may be a mouthful to swallow since it seems to fly in the face of all we have been taught, but the image of the unchanging and ponderous Supreme Being we have been taught is God does not fit with what Jesus— or any of the masters— tried to tell us over the years. If God is joy made manifest and so much of the joy in this universe is based upon discovery and learning fresh perspectives of life, how can we not consider God to be a vibrant being? God has been dancing the dance of life throughout eternity, sending forth rays of creation constantly, and reveling in the possibilities that are constantly being created.

And so we have our very being, our essence, our personification (image) of God, slowed down to include what we call time. We are now made with a nature of light (our soul) and a nature of dark (our shadow), creating a seemingly dual nature built to experience joy and sorrow, for without the dark, how can we know the light? Unless we have differences, we have no measure of what is. How do I know I am tall unless shorter people exist? Unless I know pain, how do I know comfort? Our lives are a series of comparisons. Babies have a very limited sense of differences, but adults understand millions of differences, including good from bad and everything in between.

The Shadow

Jung developed the concept of the shadow to introduce the spiritual side of our consciousness into Sigmund Freud's structural model of the psyche. One of the best books to read on the shadow is *The Shadow Effect* by Deepak Chopra, Debbie Ford, and Marianne Williamson. It explains in understandable language how important the shadow is to a well-rounded human psyche. The shadow sees differences and pushes us to have compassion. It helps us reach that next steps in our quests for the highest version of the highest vision we have ever had for ourselves.

Without the shadow, we would have no function in the plan of God that Jesus talked about. Why would we heal the sick, help the poor, or do any of the things Jesus and the other masters talked about? We can appreciate what we are seeing through our own experiences. Because we have what we call the shadow, we can appreciate the poor and have compassion for the destitute or the ill.

One of principle tasks in life is to know our shadows, accept them for the proper roles they can have in our lives, and use the shadow in the positive manner it was meant to be used. Without the negative experiences of my life, I would not be writing about these steps. I learned the original twelve steps of AA while fighting a problem that threatened all I held dear. I learned the secrets of comfort and wellness that the original twelve steps presented. My mentor in the 12 steps, Tom Powers, studied the twelve steps under the direct guidance of Bill Wilson, the founder of Alcoholics Anonymous. Bill, as he was known, considered the 12 steps a direct dictation from God, and he wrote them in one sitting and reportedly never modified them. As one of the teachers in my life, Tom gave me many insights into the richness of thought that the twelve steps represent.

Like when you sit in front of a fire in winter. You don't have to be smart or anything. The fire warms you.
—Desmond Tutu

The shadow is a true gift from God. It is not a mistake. God does not make mistakes. How can I state that when we know the pain the shadow causes us? The pain represents growth and life experiences, which are the very essence of life or God (Life is another name for God.). We must understand that pain and loss help us join with God, for we must experience the negative to appreciate the positive. We can see the flow of life that supports all and provides the strength and support at times of pain and loss. It permits us to move forward in times of physical, mental, or spiritual pain. "No Pain, no Gain" is an old maxim that we toss off, but without pain and suffering and humiliation we do not grow. So welcome the unwelcome, and use those painful moments as a means for growth.

God is love.

As we grow in maturity of love, we begin to understand the enormity of what we say when we say *"God is love"* (1 John 4:16, ESV). This is referenced in many parts of the Bible. We cry to God, *"How could this happen? If God is love, how can so much pain be in our world? How can I suffer so?"* Pain is such a part of our lives. We find it extremely difficult to believe that "God is love." My personal experience is that only by surrendering ourselves into the love of God can we begin to understand that God is love personified. Understanding and falling into that embrace allows me to say that God has never let me down.

I have come to understand and accept as part of my creation my Shadow, and yes, I put that out with a capital letter because it is the one part, if not the most important part of my life, that has let me see how deeply God loves me. Through my shadow I have experienced forgiveness, especially on the receiving side, which permits me to forgive others with surprising ease. Through my shadow I can see, and accept and forgive, the shadow of others. I have come to understand the beauty of our seemingly flawed lives, not as being flawed, but as perfection, where we grow and evolve through the interaction of the light and dark of our lives. Without the shadow in our lives, we would be a one dimensional being, unable to express the beauty of God that underlies all we do, for we would not have the seemingly duality of life to understand who we are.

Yes, God is love, and we are made in that image of God, so that we too are love. Our purpose in life is to discover that we are love, with as much love in our very being as our souls, that image of God, can hold. As a part of the infinite ocean of God, even though we are only a wavelet of that ocean, we are love. The shadow in our lives opens us up to experience that love in a unique way that only I can feel and absorb, as you are able to feel the unique way that God is love in your life, by the forgiveness and the various attributes of your version of your shadow.

The shadow for each of us is as unique as our very being. The complexities of our shadow is ours alone, each individual, like the preverbal snowflake, no two ever alike. That is why all descriptions of the shadow can be only a general description, for each one of us is unique, and while common descriptions can be used such as anger, resentments, etc., the varying levels and details are always different, always forming a unique picture of our individuality.

And yet, we are the same; we are all part of the one being. We all contain the same general patterns, angers, resentments, our ego's drives, etc. No one avoids having all these parts of our psyche, even though they differ greatly in each.

So celebrate your shadow! Celebrate our oneness in being, and celebrate our uniqueness, that part of us that requires each one of us to find our own unique path to perfection. It is the part of us that permits us to see perfection and understand it as perfection. Without the gift of the shadow we would be blinded to all the uniqueness of our being and our universe, and we would not be what our Creator intended.

A Native American said this: "Inside of me there are
two dogs. One of the dogs is mean and evil.
The other dog is good. The mean dog fights
The good all the time." When asked which
Dog wins, he reflected for a moment. Then
Said: "The one I feed the most."'
—Anonymous

Step 7. We acknowledge both the light and dark elements of our nature as to who we are in the deeper reality of our being.

Questions to Ponder

Look at your predilections, tendencies and life approaches, as stated in your written Step 4, and see your shadow and how it acts out in your life.

Write down how these tendencies in your life direct your life, and see how you can redirect these approaches to life to work for your growth rather than working for your limitations, for these characteristics of your life can be your strengths.

Meditation

My Eternal Wisdom, your gift to me, our created self in this passage through physicality is perfection, including that portion of myself that seems to be so negative. I accept all that you created as myself, and marvel, how after passing through what appears to be painful events, I can see the growth potential in each event, not despite the pain, but *because* of the pain. I grow mostly through these negative experiences that make me stretch myself far and wide beyond my comfort zone, and I thank you profoundly for these opportunities to grow in your love. My profound gratitude for the shadow side of my being allows me to see Your perfection in the creation of this person that I have become, and I bow my head in gratitude and love for my life which has been so rich in forgiveness and love as a result of the shadow that has enriched my life.

Chapter 26

Step 8

If you are bringing your gift to the altar, and there remember that your brother or your sister has anything against you, go first and be reconciled to him or her, and then come back and present your gift.
—Matthew 5:23-24, Paraphrased from several translations

Step 8. We take responsibility for our choices that have unintended consequences, including creating pain for others and ourselves.

Taking responsibility for our actions is an important part of growing in maturity. We cannot control what other people will do or their reaction to our actions, but we have full control of our own actions and reactions. No matter what the provocation, our response is our own response, and we bear full responsibility for our actions.

This step is surprisingly hard to live up to since it is an ongoing process that never ceases. It becomes easier to follow the more often we accept our responsibility, but it always remains one of the sore points. It makes us face our negative actions, especially those actions that have injured others (at least in our own minds).

Many times, we need a little bit of time between the time of our action, the recognition of the exact nature of what we did, and our acceptance of responsibility for our action. After spending many decades, I finally have found it easier to accept my own part of the problem. Within a few minutes I can usually accept my role in an issue. It does get easier with practice, and I have had plenty of practice.

The Instinctual Center

The instinctual or moving center of the mind is the part just above the central nervous system. It is commonly called the fight-or-flight part of the brain. It also contains the sexual side of the mind, which is why that drive is so difficult to control for most people. The reaction time for this center is extremely short—a few milliseconds—and almost impossible to stop. When we touch something hot, we immediately pull back without having to think. Herein lies all of our fears, terrors, and defense mechanisms we use when we feel we are under attack.

Most of our problems arise in the instinctual center. I am assuming you are basically a decent person and do not go out of your way to provoke or annoy others. Otherwise, you would not be reading this treatise. The instinctual center in our lives causes us all problems. The fight-or-flight center is always alert for the slightest perceived problem that may arise, and it triggers alarm bells in the brain that raise blood pressure, cause people to go on full alert, sends out adrenaline, and destroys peace of mind in one fell swoop.

The task we have before us is to teach the instinctual center that the world is not going to end because someone said or did something. This training will usually take years, and it only ends when we become masters or we transition. Nothing that occurs is out of place, and all is well in God's world, whether it appears that way to the outside observer or not.

Jesus could face his death with a calmness that said, "This is a necessity, and it is okay." *"Father, forgive them, for they do not know what they are doing."* (Luke 23:34, NIV)

The Emotional Center

The emotional center—how we react to what we perceive—also acts with amazing speed, but not as fast as the instinctive center. There is little or no time between what we observe and what we feel. The emotional center is directly driven by the instinctual center and causes us untold grief because of our seemingly instinctual responses of anger and fear. One of the differences between the instinctual center and the emotional center is that we can have better control over the emotional center than the instinctual center.

The instinctual center is controlled almost entirely by environmental background, and it reacts as it will react. The emotional center can be trained to respond differently, and this is one of the traits of a master. The emotional center is under control of higher centers of a master, and it will not respond in error. Jesus had full control of his responses to the events in his life, and he did not respond beyond the level of response required by the immediate action. Sometimes that reaction was firm and swift—as with the moneychangers in the temple—but even there, he was careful not inflict permanent damage. He spilled the coins on the floor, but they could be picked up. He drove the flocks out, but they could be found and retrieved. He told those with doves for sacrifice to leave since driving the doves out of the cages would have meant a loss for the owners. Even in this display of anger, he was careful to avoid long-term loss.

Depending on your disposition, your control of your emotions is a positive sign or a sign of inner terror. Only if you feel that your outward response is always a measure of the event can you say you have true control. I still find myself biting out something in anger or frustration when it would be far better to listen and think before responding, but my emotional center is still way too volatile for my own best interests.

Thinking Center

In the thinking center, we have a better chance to function. It gives us a chance to respond with grace. The thinking center takes time to respond, often several seconds. In the meantime, our instinctive and emotional centers run all over the place, causing us pain and wreaking havoc in our vicinity. When the thinking center catches up with what we have said, the damage is done. We need to stop, accept what we did, and make amends for our actions. Thus, our energies have created pain for others and pain for ourselves in the process.

These are our actions.

This is the time to own up and accept what we have already done. The words and actions are out there, and there is nothing we can do to pull them back. We accept that we did something, apologize, and move on. Hopefully we did not do harm to the extent that it hurts the relationship, but if we apologize and move on, we can change. The other person then should learn to look beyond and forgive.

Forgiveness

And now comes the other shoe. What do we do if the other person said or did something that hurt us? Peter asked Jesus how many times to forgive another. Jesus said, *"I do not say seven times, but seventy times seven"* (Matt: 18:22, NASB). There is no limit to how many times we should forgive another.

We do not forgive another person for his or her sake, but for ours. Mahatma Gandhi said, *"The weak can never forgive. Forgiveness is the attribute of the strong."* These quotes, and many more of similar nature, lead us to understand that forgiveness is a sign of strength—even more than an apology—but both acts are signs of strength. No relationship can last unless both parties are willing to forgive and put the action and reaction aside. Unless we value our relationship above the perceived slight, real or imagined, the relationship cannot survive.

The choice to forgive others for the pain they may have caused us is paramount to accepting the forgiveness of our misdeeds. *"Forgive us our debts, as we also have forgiven our debtors."* We cannot forgive ourselves for the pain we have caused others without forgiving others for the pain they have caused us.

Once we forgive others, we must seek forgiveness from them. We must ask forgiveness when necessary to mend any friction between us.

Taking Responsibility for our Actions

Take responsibility for actions that can injure others or ourselves. No action that injures another leaves us unscarred. Only by accepting our actions as our own actions, intended or not, can we grow in love and being. We recognize that we are responsible for what we say or do. Each of us carries our own responsibility, including the responsibility to learn to stop ourselves before we do

> *It is a painful thing to look at your own trouble and know that you yourself and no one else has made it.*
> *—Sophocles*

something we will regret. Gaining control of our reactions and emotional response is a lifelong commitment that is often too slow to come and hard to maintain.

What have others to say about this? Albert Einstein said, *"Man must cease attributing his problems to his environment, and learn again to exercise his will— his personal responsibility."* Sophocles said, *"It is a painful thing to look at your own trouble and know that you yourself and no one else has made it."*

The choice is ours.

Only by taking responsibility for our actions and places in life can we hope to change what and where we are. One of the principle purposes of these twelve steps is to recognize that we are responsible for our states of mind and places we find ourselves. We are solely responsible for our places in life, and by changing our perspectives, we change our places in this life. We can have a life of abundance, that is, a life filled with joy and inner peace and strength, but we understand that the choice of that place is ours and ours alone. We can choose to remain buried in the mire of self-pity, bemoaning our fate, and that fate will continue. We can also choose to have fates filled with light and joy, despite what is going on in our lives.

Once we have new perspectives on our lives, we will find that the outer circumstances will change to accommodate our new perspectives. Sometimes the change will be subtle. Christopher Reeve had to deal with the consequences of his actions, but the love gained from his wife and family and the whole acting community was a priceless gift to his sense of peace and joy, which was evident in his interviews toward the end of his life.

Usually, we have not constrained ourselves to the point that Christopher Reeve did, and we should have no problem to have a much more positive outlooks on life than we have had. The purpose of these twelve steps is to bring us into lives of abundance, and that requires us to change our perspectives on life and accept that we are responsible for our states in life.

The eighth step is another key point in the road to abundance: only by accepting that we are responsible for each thing we do in our lives will we be able to move to the point that we understand that we can make different choices that will lead to different results.

Consequences

We bear the consequences of our actions. The consequences of the actions we have taken have formed into physicality and can no longer be changed. All future actions, stemming from those actions and their consequences, can be changed. Future actions can lead us to abundance, and the consequences of these actions will somewhat alleviate the original, sometimes devastating consequences, such as granting Christopher Reeve new opportunities and starting a foundation to help quadriplegics.

These movements of grace that follow from lives of abundance are part of the evolution of life. We are creating the next highest version of the highest vision we've ever had of ourselves, and the visions are for the entire human race. Part of the task we came to in this cycle of physicality is to help raise the entire human race to the next level of existence—one life at a time, starting with our own. Only by changing ourselves can we change the human race, and by changing ourselves, we introduce a higher set of energy levels to all around us—and to the entire human race.

A life of abundance, while certainly meaningful to me as an individual, is part of the overall drive of the human race to change so that all humans can live in abundance.

Admitting mistakes is not a weakness;
on the contrary,
it shows an openness of your heart.
It takes guts to say sorry.
—Vishwas Chavan

Step 8. We take responsibility for our choices that have unintended consequences, including creating pain for others and ourselves.

Questions to Ponder

In your life, where have you hurt another with words or actions that should not have been said?

Write down what these events included, and the person to whom we did them to, and look at the pain you caused another for whatever reason.

Be prepared to tell the other person your sorrow for injuring them—and be prepared to ask for forgiveness.

Take action for your own peace of mind. This action must be taken as a true token of sorrow for our actions—and should never be taken when it will injure another or bring pain to another. Always define your motivation before acting.

Meditation

My Eternal Wisdom, I place my life in your hands. I have surrendered myself into your shelter, and I accept responsibility for the good and the not so good that I do so that I may understand the energies you hold out to me as being rightfully mine. With these energies that are mine, I can step into that blessed life you have promised: a life of abundance. I give this life back to you, God, to raise all of humanity to the next level of being. I bow in gratitude for this opportunity to live in service, joy, and peace. When the time comes for me to leave this plane and join more fully with your being, I will move with joy to that stage of life.

Chapter 27

Step 9

Give and it will be given to you.
They will pour into your lap a good
measure—pressed down, shaken together,
and running over.
For by your standards of measure,
it will be measured to you in return.
—Luke 6:38, NASB

Step 9. We commit to a life of healing and transformation. Through our thoughts, words, and actions, we will demonstrate who we are in truth.

O nce we have surrendered our thoughts and actions to God, we will start to live in new ways. This can have profound implications in the way we treat our families, our friends, our acquaintances, and ourselves. We begin to act as one who has the abundance of God already in his or her being. We can portray ourselves as people in love with life and love itself.

This step, like all the others, takes a lifetime of application before it becomes second nature. That is part of our very existence. We can change the way we treat those around us, and we will discover that we are one being, each of us displaying a different facet of God. Our lives will be different when we connect with the life of abundance, and the life of abundance is ours for the asking. All we must do is ask and follow our hearts when we ask. The steps become part of who we are, and they become a part of who we will be in our next lives. In this step, we begin to demonstrate who we are—internally and externally.

We are the image of God.

For some of us, this step will be simple. For those of us whose hearts are already in the path of healing and transformation, this step is simple. If our hearts are giving, we look carefully at who we are and the way we present ourselves to other people.

A difficult trait that sometimes appears, not what I am talking about in this step, is giving of ourselves to others to the point where we effectively cease to exist. All we think about is pleasing others, and that is not who we are. That kind of doormat, for that is what this person has become, is a people pleaser whose very being is submerged in a world of fear and self-hatred. Yes, self-hatred. Do we not believe that we have nothing of worth to offer? Do we not believe that our opinions have no merit?

This is not the creation of God we were meant to be. When we start to transform ourselves into a creation that expresses the life of abundance, we must realize that God created this wonderful being that is who we are. We are created in the image and likeness of God, a being like God that has an eternal soul whose likeness is God. We are capable of arranging our lives to be full of joy and love—one with our Creator. This is our created being, the essence of who we are. Who are we to deny what God has created?

Some people are at the opposite end of the scale. Know-it-alls and the ones whose bluster and demands dominate a group can cause endless problems for their friends. There are many variations of this, including the overly talkative person and those who brook no challenge to their entrenched way of thinking. These include those who dominate conversations, do not permit others to speak their opinions, and do not tolerate the thoughts of others. If your life tends in this direction, you learn to listen and treat others' thoughts as your own. Their thoughts contain messages from God, and we need to hear them—no matter how different or oblivious they seem.

No matter where we find ourselves in the grand scheme of things, we listen to our souls' desires and place value on them. We see if our present thinking is so desirable that we are willing to live on as our present lives are leading us.

Most of the time, our lives are somewhat chaotic. We try to find peace in our lives when they are more chaotic than normal, which drives us to look for answers that will help resolve the future. The search is for a balanced future, where fears, worries, and concerns can be alleviated with hope for the future and abundance.

What we seek, we must give.

This step presents a great discovery: what we seek is what we must give away. If we seek lives of healing and transformation, we give others healing and transformation. If we seek lives of abundance, we must seek to give others abundance in their lives. To ease pain where we find it and cause healing in others, we need healing in ourselves. To give to others is to receive the same. This is the great conundrum of spiritual lives. Only by giving to others what we seek will we discover that we already have what we seek.

Jesus said, *"Give and it will be given to you. They will pour into your lap a good measure—pressed down, shaken together, and running over. For by your standards of measure it will be measured to you in return"* (Luke 6:38, NASB).

Jesus summed up clearly what we must do to live a life of abundance: Give, and give freely to all that seek. This is the life of healing and transformation that we have described in step 9. When we seek to give to others—and others will be in our lives for this purpose—we will discover that when we give to others, we will have more for ourselves than before. God has promised this, and God is always true to God's promises.

In a direct message from God, Neale Donald Walsch wrote, *"Instead of searching for someone to love you, be someone who could be loved. Send what you wish to receive. Be what you wish to experience. This is the greatest secret in all of life. Be what you are looking for, and what you are looking for will find you."*

Deepak Chopra said, when tweeted with the question, *"How do I find the right one?"* replied, *"Stop looking for the right one. Be the right one."*

Is this not what Jesus said in Luke? We will receive all we asked for, pressed down, shaken together, and running over, for what we offer others is what we will receive.

Again: Made in the Image of God

This phrase has been called the most quoted phrase in the Bible. But what has been missing is the meaning of that phrase, from looking at the nature of God. The one feature of God that is most clear is that God

The image of God infused in us never sees the light of day in the service of self, but it becomes the light of day in the service of others.
—Craig D. Lounsbrough

is first and foremost a Creator, a lover. He creates and constantly recreates the universe and all that exists as an act of love. God's love requires fresh creation and a life of vibrant love as intense as that first blush of infatuation that occurs when two soulmates meet. Where do we think the heady sensation comes from? The impact between two souls faintly mirrors the intensity of love that God radiates for all eternity. We are immersed in the love of God. There is never any moment when God's love is not who we are. We are an individualized part of that love. We are brought here under the illusion of being separate so that we may discover that heady sensation of being love from a fresh perspective.

Who We Are

It is time to become aware of who we are. We are too often fearful cowards, afraid to look at our lives. The fates batter us at times, but our exteriors are brave fronts. Inside, we all recognize that we are afraid and alone. No matter how close we attempt to get to another, we are still isolated individuals who nobody knows. Our dark secrets are locked up inside, causing us pain and shame.

These steps are designed to help us release those secrets in steps 4 and 5, give them to God in step 6, and accept our shadows as a critical part of our being in steps 7 and 8. In step 9, we are asked to discover the wonder of the created beings that we are. This step starts us on the path to the wonder children that we were created to be.

The Wonder Child

You are a wonder child, capable of creating a world around you that is a paradise on earth. The gates to paradise were never closed; our eyes were blinded from seeing paradise all around us. What made paradise? It was not the description made on physical terms of great weather, balmy trees, food everlasting, and the freedom to walk around naked. Those were exterior trappings used to describe the incredible reality that one could see God face to face. Was that seeing a physical reality? No. God cannot be described in any one physical manner. Open your eyes and look around you. Everything you see with your physical eyes and your interior feelings is God. God can be seen by looking into the eyes of another human. Look into the eyes of a child, look at the sunset, look at the hills, look at a flower, and look at the next house. If you have eyes to see, you are looking at God!

God is the All in All, the Alpha and the Omega. There is nothing that is not God. If there anything that was not God, then God would not be the All in All. God has no needs and no demands. God said to Moses, *"I am who I am"* (Exodus 3:14, NIV).

God is your neighbor. God is the drunk in the gutter. God is the killer in the hills.

Jesus said, *"And God said 'Whatever you did to the least of these brothers and sisters of mine, you did it to me'"* (Matt 25:40, New American Standard Version, gender neutral).

Jesus tried his best to tell us that God is all that there is, but his vocabulary and the ability of his listeners to understand was limited. We will never know all the wonderful things Jesus said because his words were not written down for more than forty years after his death, and much more was forgotten than was remembered.

You are in paradise.

We do have the ability of live in paradise, and you can see God. You carry the kingdom of God within you, as promised by Jesus. All you do is step into that kingdom, which is always within you, waiting for your call. That is the life of abundance. That is the life we can achieve by claiming who we are—back from the blind and self-centered beings we were at the start. We all have more room to grow. Few of us are masters like Jesus and the Buddha. Unless you are a master, you are blind and self-centered.

This path is meant for all of humanity, but we are to go on this path according to the talents and the journey that we were created to be.

This is who we are.

> **"Why is anyone lovable—
> if it be not that God put (God's) love
> into each of us?"**
> **Fulton J. Sheen**

Step 9. We commit to a life of healing and transformation. Through our thoughts, words, and actions, we will demonstrate who we are in truth.

Questions to Ponder

Do you see yourself able to live in paradise, that kingdom of God that lies within, where you can see the face of God in all that is around you?

Write down your thoughts on the concept of being able to live in the kingdom of God that lies within you.

The world we seem to live in is messy, chaotic, frightening, and certainly nothing at all like what we imagine paradise should be. How can God call this turmoil paradise? How do we reconcile this with the promise of Jesus?

Write down how you see the kingdom of God reconciling with the actuality of the world around us, putting your perceptual take on the world up to be taken by God into a new vision.

Meditation

My Eternal Wisdom, take me by the hand and guide me gently into the awareness of who I truly am. I understand I am a part of your being. Open my heart so that I may know that I am your child, a part of your DNA, a vital part unlike any other creation in this universe or any other universe. I bow my head for this opportunity for my soul to sing your song, that I am sustained by your love, as it says in *A Course in Miracles*. I ask your guidance as I feel my way into this world so that I may express myself more and more as a guiding light to follow your star into paradise here on earth.

Chapter 28

Step 10

*If you only knew what God has in the book
of success for you,
you wouldn't have a single reason to live in
doubts and worries again.*
—Edmund Mbiaka

Step 10. We continue to examine our lives and pursue a spiritual solution by surrendering to God.

*L*iving in abundance is a process that takes the entire journey of life, one day at a time. The effort does require maintenance since the process either moves forward or in reverse. There is no middle ground where stasis is achieved and one can forget about it, and it will just continue.

It stops and shrinks and vanishes or grows—one day at a time.

Life is growth.

During a recent discussion at church, I mentioned that I am always seeking to become a higher version of myself. At my age, the standard rules and regulations of behavior no longer held sway over my life.

Someone asked, "Are you still trying to decide what you want to be when you grow up?"

I said, "If the definition of growing up is to become rigid and unchanging, I will never grow up. When I pass from this life, I expect to continue to grow and change."

If I had stopped when stepping back from my engineering life, which most consider an unqualified success, I would not be writing these words to help (hopefully) at least one person find joy and peace in a life of abundance.

I have seen this reluctance to engage in long-term change in every program I have ever seen. First, there is exhilaration and discovery, and then the world gets in the way. The kids have to go here or there, bills have to be paid, and work becomes more pressing. There is always something. I watch people become excited, easily find the time to make the effort, and then the effort becomes too much. Things interfere. There is always a reason.

Life returns to its chaotic beginning, and the dream of a life of abundance (or a life free of alcohol, free of drugs, etc.) diminishes. The same old life and drudgeries appear; only dreams and fond memories of what could have been remain.

The last three steps lead to life everlasting. Life can bring lasting joy and happiness into our lives, and nothing can upset it. This life will carry us through to the next. Joy and peace will swell into one crescendo after another. It will culminate when we pass and see God face to face, in full glory.

Life is good.

These are big promises, but God has said many times that this is the result. Why do we question this expectation and doubt the result? Many people understand that the promises are true. The twelve-step program has helped millions find sobriety, and this basic approach can be used to find joy and happiness in your own life—free from the fears and concerns that corner us in despair, fear, and worry.

Jesus said, *"Give and it will be given to you. They will pour into your lap a good measure—pressed down, shaken together, and running over"* (Luke 6:38, NASB).

This program gives to others, and we immerse ourselves into the balm of God's words, music, and beauty every day. They offer us succor to ease our pain and concerns.

One cannot live partially in a life of God's way. One either gives oneself fully into the loving arms of God—or does not. If not, life

> *He who has a why to live for can bear almost any how.*
> *—Nietzsche*

will return to its meaningless chores with some joy and much pain.

The process is rewarding unto itself. If we apply ourselves as well as we can with this program, the result will flow into our lives and encourage us to try more until we suddenly realize that our lives lead to happiness—despite the outward appearances that may still be present.

We will carry the consequences of our previous life as reminders of what it took to get us to that point and provide the knowledge to help others who appear in your life.

I have seen and experienced it countless times.

Examining Your Life

A funny thing happened on the way to the forum. After completing the previous steps, we feel freer than at any time in our lives. We have told our secrets, and we feel as if all is over. When our lives continue, we still find that we react in the same old ways, causing many of the same old problems. We wonder what happened, but we find that the instinctual center is still responding in old ways. It will seem like these reactions are built into our psyches in a way that we cannot prevent destructive behavior.

Your personality type will indicate which negative reactions you carry with you. The way we react to situations gives us insights into how to manage our shadows so that they provide us with guidance and do not overwhelm us. The shadow is important and helps us see the beauty of life by revealing the counterpoint of our dark side, giving us a measuring point to see where we are. Thus our shadow allows us to know good from bad, grace from evil, giving us joy when we overcome part of the dark impulses that seem to overwhelm us at times, or sorrow when we follow the dark side of our being.

The Highest Vision of Life

I talked about setting up a vision of ourselves. We try to live up to the next highest version of the next highest vision we have of ourselves. The constant striving to see a more perfect version of ourselves and trying to live up to that vision keep us growing and learning. The process never stops. We can see greater possibilities rising up in front of us as God opens our eyes to the greater glories in this life. He brings us the joy and happiness we seek. Joy is ours for the asking, and it is always present.

We can stretch ourselves a little more to reach our goals. This effort requires some time, and it is usually best at the end of the day. We can look at where we have met our goals and where we could have been a little more compassionate, especially with loved ones. This is not a time for self-flagellation, finger-pointing, or accepting defeat. It is a time for observation. Note the areas where a different response would have worked better. This is not a judgment time; it is a reflection time. Try to figure out ways to use better responses in similar situations.

It will occur. Count on it.

Pursuing a Spiritual Solution

Pierre Teilhard de Chardin said, *"We are not physical beings having a spiritual experience; we are spiritual beings having a physical experience."* Almost all of us live as if we are physical beings having the occasional spiritual experience. He said that this life is not who we are. We have let ourselves be fooled by what we believe we are seeing. We are limited only by the perceptual limits of the physical world that we can sense and our physical interpretations of the world.

De Chardin had it right. We are spiritual beings *"made in the image and likeness of God"* (Genesis 1). The entire works of Jesus are based upon that statement in Genesis, the most quoted phrase in the Bible. We are spiritual beings in the image and likeness of God. God has no one physical form—but all physical forms, including dark matter and dark energy, and far beyond. God still has the infinite power of creation within. If we are to become that new being, we forge ourselves anew in the image we have sensed but not fully accepted. When we accept who we are, spiritual beings filled with the spirit of God, that kingdom of

God that lies within, we can begin to understand the potential power that is ours for the choosing.

Reclaiming Your Birthright

In some ways, "pursuing a spiritual solution" does not state the meaning of what we are doing. We are reclaiming our spiritual beings, which leads us to abundance. By reclaiming, we state that we are the creators of our lives—one with our Creator and made in the image of the universe.

We are laying claim to our very birthright, the innermost part of our being. We have the right to shine in the heavens as beings of God and create the life of joy and happiness that can be ours. This can result in changes to the way we live. God will always grant us lives of joy.

Surrendering to Your God

The act of reclaiming your birthright as a Creator in your own right is the act of surrendering to the arms of God.

Jesus said, *"Greater works than this shall you do"* (John 14:12). We hold the power to create our lives to bring us joy and happiness, and we will be joined by the essence of who we are to reach that level of confidence.

Our lives can be overwhelming and threaten everything we have. When this occurs, we might believe God has abandoned us. That is the very time we abandon ourselves into God and let God guide us. The most desperate times open up our being to the light of the world, our God.

These moments are the moments of surrender, and we feel so stretched that we can let our egos pause so that we reclaim our souls. These moments are a gift from God. Dependence on the physical world is not enough for us. We must let it go and be with God to find solace in the Eternal Source.

Let it go. Our souls will claim our beings, and we can live in the joy of God. This feeling of joy may be a momentary respite, but it is there for us to claim any time we wish. God will melt the pain in your hearts, bring relief, and show you the joy that awaits if you surrender your ego to the care of God.

This is why so many members of Alcoholics Anonymous would never give up what they have found in the love of God. They live continuously in the joy of God. They recognize the pain they have caused to others and to themselves, but they believe the joy they have found could not have been found through any other means.

Do not despair if you find yourself buried in the mire of life. In this mire, you will find the gift of life. The wall separating your life from God is only a film, easily torn apart, and the act of letting your life rest into God is the relief you have searched for all of your life.

Do not despair if the problem still exists the day after releasing it—or even the next minute. This act of surrendering and finding your soul is an ongoing process. One day, the pain will end—even if the condition that caused it does not end—and you will find yourself in the joy of God. The event will end someday, but the joy you have found will never end.

"The salvation of humanity is through love and in love."
Viktor Frankl, *Man's Search for Ultimate Meaning*

Step 10. We continue to examine our lives and pursue a spiritual solution by surrendering to God.

Questions to Ponder

Look at your life over the past week. How does that time compare with having a life of abundance? Write down how this week has flowed and open up to asking for forgiveness where necessary.

Do you see the freshness of love in the form of joy and peace filling your being, especially during your daily quiet time with God?

Write down your sense of the presence of God during your quiet time.

Meditation

Oh, Eternal Wisdom, I bow in humble gratitude for these opportunities you offer in my life—as desperate as they seem. I recognize and want to take advantage of the opportunities they offer me to find my soul, that part of my being that is the image of you. I place myself in your service to be of help to those you put into my path, so that they too may find the joy of your presence in their lives as I have found in my own life. Open me up to the opportunities in this life of joy. Bring me into alignment with the universal flow of your energy so that I may be more aware each day of your love, which is the center of my life.

Chapter 29

Step 11

Prayer is not asking.
It is a longing of the soul.
It is a daily admission of one's weakness.
It is better in prayer to have
A heart without words
Than words without a heart.
—Mahatma Gandhi

Step 11. We commit to using various forms of prayer and meditation to increase our conscious contact with God, praying only for the knowledge of God's desires for us and our willingness to carry that out.

This step forms the methodology to be able to live a life of abundance on an ongoing basis. Here is where we form the lifelong habits that will enable us to grow in the recognition of the love of our God. We either grow or we diminish; there is no resting point where "That is good enough".

The life that we are learning to become was expressed several times by Jesus. *"Truly I say to you, if anyone says to this mountain, 'Go, throw yourself into the sea,' and does not doubt, but believe in their heart that what they say is going to happen, it will be granted them"* (Mark 11:23, Paraphrased from several translations).

The key part of this saying by Jesus is *"does not doubt, but believe in their heart that what they say is going to happen."* Jesus is saying that we have the creative ability to create joy, happiness, and peace in our lives—if we are willing to remove the doubts we have.

We are filled with doubt about the love of God. How many times did we pray for something that did not happen? (Actually, it may have happened the way we prayed for it to happen. We may have prayed for the wrong thing to happen.) The doubt lingers. We have heard that we are made in the image of God, and we understand that God is the Creator. Therefore, we should be creators, but our heart says that there is no way I am a creator. The ego frames everything with what it can see and hear and feel in the physical world. We are our own worst enemies.

In a comic strip, Pogo (look it up if you don't know Pogo) said, *"We have met the enemy, and it is us."* The process we learned from childhood has led to a life-long dependence on the physical world for all our resources of living and being. Now we must learn to depend on our God for all that is joyful, good, and whole in our life. And God will respond, as promised.

We are spiritual beings.

Pierre Teilhard de Chardin said, *"We are not physical beings having a spiritual experience; we are spiritual beings having a physical experience."* We can begin to catch a glimmer of that spiritual being *"made in the image of God"* when we dwell with a sunset, a sunrise, a flower, the light of love in our beloved's eyes, the moments when our breath caught at a painting, the sight of a newborn baby; all these moments when the spiritual side of our lives blazed forth in the soft light of beauty and love.

We have all tasted that side of life, and we strive to recapture that joy as often as we are able to. We are attempting in this program to accept that we are not only *worthy* of these moments, but we are *due* these moments of awareness because we are alive. We are capable of having these moments 24/7 if we desire it in the depths of our being. These moments are achieved by finding our souls and becoming aware of the stirrings of our souls at each moment of life. Then we can be one who does not doubt and believes in our hearts that what we say will happen.

We have all tasted this sensation. We all have the capacity to sense these moments, but our egos deny us the sense that these moments can be ours at any time.

They stem from outside of the ego—at a moment of openness to God's presence in the world. It can be seen in the beauty of nature, family, and the world outside of ourselves—in the world that has no name but swirls around our lives.

This life of paradise is ours for the asking. We commit to the process that will empower our lives to overcome the pull of the ego, the pull of the physical world that pounds at us through our five senses. The process is not difficult, taking only a few minutes each day, and the process leads us to that level of knowing (removing doubt) that enables us to live in abundance.

Living in the Past

We spend most of our lives living in the past. Everything we know is dependent on what we learned in the past. However, we too often take all we have learned and relive it over and over all the time. Our past fears, worries, and sense of lacking haunt us every day, and we seem to be unable to overcome our memories. One of the tasks on the road to a life of abundance is not to overcome the past, but to put it in the past! We learn to release the past, let it be in the past, and let it go so it no longer governs our every moment.

God is not in the past. God has no time frame, and the past, present, and future are all the same in the time sense of the All in All. God is in the frame of no time. For those living in the physical plain of existence, the past is important because of all the information we have soaked up in our lives. This part of the past is healthy, but the problem is in the way we picture the past in our minds. The past is in the past, and it cannot be changed in this lifetime.

We too often carry the past as emotional baggage, and we often relive the past over and over. The past sets the stage for the next step, but it cannot affect the present or the future – it truly is in the past. The past is what it is; we live with the consequences of the past, but we do not have to repeat it. We do not have to repeat the emotional part of the past because then the past becomes the present, and it prevents us from moving into a different future. The past holds us captive in its grip of fear, anger, and worries. When we relive the past emotionally, we remain frozen in those moments.

When the past has frozen us, it is best that we implement the early steps, especially steps 4 and 5: review our lives, talk to trusted friends, and let it go.

Living in the Future

We often combine living in the past with living in the future—where we will have our revenge on the past. Or we may remain frozen in fear from all the what-ifs that may occur—but probably will not occur. When we live in those moments that will *never* happen, we are unable to do the things we need to do to ease the moment that *is* happening and set us on a path to a life of abundance. The future holds the unknown, but the future is ours to set the tone for a life of abundance. How we view the future, with fear or without doubt, as Jesus put it, is the difference between *"telling the mountain to hurl into the sea"* and wallowing, frozen, in our fears of what may happen. Those fears will remain within us, for who knows, *"it may happen tomorrow"*, unless we learn to live in the present.

Living in the Moment

Living in the moment—or the now, as Eckhart Tolle puts it—does not negate all our knowledge. Instead, it puts that knowledge to use—where and when it benefits the task we are trying to accomplish. We put it aside when it will hinder the task we are trying to accomplish. We view each day as a series of events, each with its own meaning and leading to another event in our lives.

Event is not just a term. If we can make ourselves look at the day as a series of events— some pleasant and some not so pleasant—we have a chance to gain some control over our reactions to these events. Otherwise we become trapped in the event and

> *The sage is like heaven and earth: To him none are especially dear, Nor is there anyone he disfavors. He gives and gives, without condition, Offering his treasures to everyone.*
> —Tao Te Ching

cannot let it go. We react badly when the next event comes along, leading to feeling overwhelmed as the events pile up.

The boss jumped on me for some trivial incident. My spouse cheated (again) on me. The kids are holy terrors and cannot be controlled. I am finding it difficult to pay my bills. Someone close to me passed away and left a huge void.

I could go on for pages, but these events mark the daily flow of our lives in great and small ways. Some of these events have profound effects on our lives, but most of them have no lasting effect on our lives. Unless we drag them with us, they will be gone and forgotten. Usually in a very short time, we will not even recall the event that seemed so huge at the time.

When we store these events away and learn to create the calmness that this approach to life will elicit, we begin the move that leads to a life of abundance. We will understand that God will never give us more then we can hold. God desires only good things for us—beauty and joy each day of our lives.

I commit to using various forms of prayer and meditation to increase my awareness of my conscious contact with God.

Gaining a sense of control over our lives comes from spending time with our Source and feeling comfortable with that Source.

Not just when we feel like it, but each day.

Every day.

Always.

We will begin to see that God is not just our friend— but as our lover. God never lets us down, is always ready to listen and talk with us, guiding us gently but firmly if we open our inner eyes. *"For the kingdom of God lies within"* (Luke 17:21, English Revised Version).

The soul has eyes that see all levels of vibration— not the narrow spectrum that our physical senses see, feel, hear, taste, and touch. The "God spectrum" is in contact with Eternal Wisdom and can receive and respond to that level of consciousness.

Usually that level of consciousness requires a quiet time to be processed. We can get away from the sounds or the cacophony of life. This is often difficult, but once we set up such a space and time, we will look forward to our quiet time.

Finding the time is a matter of priority. We can always find the time for something we need to do or deeply desire. This is one of those moments where we choose. Do we want a life of the joy of God? Is this TV show more important? What are our goals in life? These questions may seem trivial, but our actions reveal the answers. Other matters often seem more important. They crowd in and block out that time we thought we had reserved for quiet time.

I know a young man with a busy family who are always on the go. He found himself in too many situations that he deemed harmful for himself and harmful to his family. He had to rise at six to start the family day right, and he set his alarm for five to have the quiet time he felt he needed to be able to treat his family in the right manner.

It can be done if we deem it important enough. That is the key to finding happiness in life. We make it the priority in our lives. If we find true happiness in our lives, our families will be happy, our jobs will flow more smoothly, and our lives will change. You would be surprised by how many times most of us see only the negative in our lives. We do not see the many beautiful things that occur, including the very gift of life itself. When you wake in the morning, do you thank God for the joy of life? If you so desire, you can see the gift of life in all that is around you.

Deepak Chopra said, *"If someone asks me how long they should meditate, I state, 'Meditate once a day for twenty minutes.' If they reply that they do not have the time to spend twenty minutes a day in meditation, I reply, "Then you need to spend twenty minutes twice a day."'*

Praying only for the knowledge of our God desires for us.

Does God have desires for me? His only desire for us is that we are happy. I know, it sounds crazy, but God desires only that we be happy. Now what about all the rules and regulations set up by religions? They fill bookshelf after bookshelf. The Bible has book after book detailing every moment of the religious and everyday life for the everyday person, most of which were (and still are) ignored by the average person.

God is love personified. Do we not want all those we love to be happy? Now, they seem to know what I should be doing – whether or not it will make me happy.

To be happy means having to follow the two great commandments of God: *"You shall love the lord your God with all your heart, and with all your strength, and with all your mind, ————-and your neighbor as yourself"* (Luke 10:27, NASB). All those volumes of rules was summed up by Jesus: *"Love God and love your neighbor."* Those words sum up God's desires for us. Only by loving God and our neighbor can we find the joy of life that is ours to grasp. These words are engraved on our hearts, and we know their truth instinctively. We require no rulebooks to follow these simple commands. When we let these simple axioms fade from our hearts, we find that we need these sets of rules.

Lao-tzu expressed it clearly in the Tao Te Ching.

> **When the greatness of the Tao is present,**
> **Action arises from one's own heart.**
> **When the greatness of the Tao is absent,**
> **Action comes from the rules**
> **Of "kindness and justice."**
> **—Dr. Wayne Dyer, *Living the Wisdom of the Tao***

And My Willingness to Carry That Out

We love God and our neighbor, but humanity keeps getting in the way. This is why we need a program to help us achieve a level of joining with our God so that we create a world of abundance. When we repeat the program, we will not have to think about the individual steps.

> *The function of prayer is not*
> *To influence God, but rather*
> *To change the nature of*
> *The one who prays.*
> *—Soren Kierkegaard*

Step 11. We commit to using various forms of prayer and meditation to increase our conscious contact with God, praying only for the knowledge of God's desires for us and our willingness to carry that out.

Questions to Ponder

Look at your life. Is it possible to find some time every day to look to God in concentrated form?

Write down how you would adjust your schedule to permit you to have time for meditation.

Do you believe that you have the innate capability to transform your inner being to one that sees joy and happiness in your existence?

Look around you. Do you see the many things you can be grateful for? Write down as many things as you can see and think of what bring you peace and joy and happiness.

Meditation

Oh God, the Whisperer of joy and abundance in my life, I thank you for all the joys you have brought into my life, and all the joys that lay before me. I know that I am transitioning from this world of physicality to the world of the Holy Spirit, where these words will blossom into an eternity of joy and love. I ask to have the scales of blindness removed from my eyes so that I may see the joy you offer to me every day of my life. I give thanks and am filled with gratitude for the many joys you offer me each day. I know that if I pursue these wonders in expectation, I will become aligned with the marvelous gifts of life.

Chapter 30

Step 12

May God break my heart so completely
That the whole world fall in.
—Mother Teresa

Step 12. We are committed to continued exploration of these sacred dimensions in our lives. We will endeavor to pass these practices and purposes to others seeking joy and happiness and practice these principles in our lives.

*I*f we wish to continue to live lives of abundance, we change our approaches to life in general and search out the meaning of life each moment. We choose openness in each moment. We explore further, every day, and be willing and eager to share our experiences with others if we are to find lasting peace and joy.

In December 1967, I was living a what I thought a happy life. I'd been married a few years. We had three daughters and were expecting another one. God spoke quite firmly to me and turned my life in a new direction.

I was not able to speak about that event for many years. I had no words to explain those few hours when God wrapped around me and lifted me into a cloud of bliss and spelled out to me that I was to follow the events that would unfold before me in the future. I would be guided when necessary in various forms, and I was to trust implicitly that God would provide for me for the rest of my life.

God has done as what was promised. I had two intensive guides right then for the next four years. A wonderful priest guided my prayer life, and a mystic guided me into the mystical path of understanding.

God led us to upstate New York from Long Island, and we have lived there on a mountaintop (ok, a high hill) for the past forty-five years. I have continued the daily time of prayer ever since that time, never letting that time lapse, despite what was going on in my life. I hit some rough spots and used the twelve-step program to gain respite and insights, and I worked daily on this way.

Seeing God

But even in the beginning, those moments of bliss did not happen out of the blue. I have had a good relationship with my God since I was a young child. Like most teenagers, I went through a spell of questioning the existence of God, but the example of my brother reaching through many difficulties during his quest for God inspired me back into a belief that grew through the years.

About three years before my awakening event, my wife and I made a Cursillo retreat, which is a powerful, witness-filled, three-day retreat. It brought my faith into full flower that has never been relinquished. I joined the leadership group of the Cursillo and received much benefit from that relationship.

Immediately after the event with God, I became aware of the glimmering concept that God had held me in the palm of his hands, sheltering me even when strong winds blew. When I lost my job in 1970, I was positive that I would find another job. My wife and I left the future in God's hands, and we opened ourselves up for what came next. My mystic guide assured me that things would go well, and I devoted myself to my new job: finding the right job.

The Sunday after being laid off there was a one-inch ad in the *New York Times* job section that seemed written for me. It took a week to write a resume and my response with the help of my wife's brother, a technical writer. I had a response in about three weeks, and in the first week in December, I ventured up to Binghamton NY for an interview.

My family and I had vacationed in that area the previous summer and fallen in love with the green rolling hills and blue waters in the region. (Coincidence? I do not think so. I call that synchronicity, a term coined by C. J. Jung, who was referring to unexplained coincidences that together formed deeper meanings.)

When a job was offered, we did not hesitate to accept. God was calling us to a new area and a new set of vocations. I started my job on the first working day of 1971. God found us a home on a mountaintop with eight acres that includes a half-acre pond, and we are still here. God has surrounded us with beauty and grace and given us a lovely home and reasonably good health.

And my prayer life has continued to this day.

And God has continued to bless us to this day.

Life problems? Yes, some were severe, but with continued faith in God, things are fine. I am blessed in this life.

I commit to continued exploration of these sacred dimensions in my life.

My day does not feel correct until I have some quiet time for prayer and meditation and some additional time for spiritual reading. My wife and I pray and meditate together for about half an hour in the morning or when we can almost every day. Sometimes things are hectic with appointments (usually doctors at our age), but we find some time during the day for prayer, either together or separate. We feel blessed that we have this time together.

We are always on the lookout for new ways to enhance our prayer time, new books from inspired authors to guide us, and other means to give us insights into the mystery of the Divine. There is always more to understand and explore, and the vista into the future is grand indeed. We will continue to endeavor to pass these practices and purposes in our lives to others seeking joy and happiness

Most of my spare time has been spent trying to pass the joy and happiness I have found to others. Shortly after coming here in 1971, the very first day in fact, I talked with a pastor who was recommended to me and introduced myself. I asked if there was a Cursillo group in Binghamton. He said I should talk with 'Dave'.

Peace is not the absence of conflict, but the presence of God no matter what the conflict.
—Anonymous

I went to evening Mass, and at the sign of peace, a tall gentleman in front of me turned around and introduced himself as "Dave." (Again, coincidence? No way! Synchronicity!) I helped start the movement in the diocese and remained lay director for more than ten years, attempting to inspire those who joined us in a consistent life of prayer and walking with confidence with God.

In the eighties, I joined a twelve-step group. My next guide, Tom Powers, was a fountain of knowledge in both twelve-step guidance and the mystical path of wisdom. This group was in a community about seventy-five miles from home. I stayed connected with that group and started several other similar groups to guide people toward a life of joy and happiness by walking a path with the Divine Wisdom by using AA's twelve-step approach. This continued for about twenty years, until Tom passed and I had to take a few months off with MERSA. The distance became too far to travel on a weekly basis or more by myself.

That led to the writing of this series. I continue to share my knowledge of the path to joy and happiness. I presently facilitate a study group of the work of Neale Donald Walsch, called "Conversation with God".

I let others know about the possibility of finding lasting joy and happiness. It saddens me when I see others searching for joy, using distraction after distraction, and not finding joy or happiness. I have used groups and movements in this process—besides talking when an opportunity arises with others—about finding joy and happiness, despite what life is.

When one attempts to teach others a topic, one always learns more than one teaches. This axiom is true for all things we teach. It is true when walking the path of God too. Every time we tell another, it firms up the truth more deeply in our hearts. It is true that these truths seem to bubble up within me, ready to burst out at a moment's notice. I am one of the fortunate ones, sensing that warmth of the God's love at the edge of my awareness.

God is one who shares. God shares life especially, filling all life with a beauty beyond comparison— whether we are aware of it or not. Walking a path with God means that we must share our physical and spiritual bounty with those around us. All who are brought into our lives are brought there for a purpose.

There are no accidents under God. He creates all so we may experience divinity on a day-to-day level. When we do not share our physical bounty or our spiritual bounty, we do not grow. We stunt the truth at that moment, becoming less than who we are. We share and grow—or we hold back and shrink. That is how life is. Life can never be static. It must always change for the better or the worse.

I was fortunate that God opened up opportunities for me to use my gifts in formal ways. If anyone is open, opportunities will abound, but the best approach is to be. If one is living on the path of God, one is always filled with a level of joy that shows on the outside and draws others to you. It is in the act of being that we grow in who we are, and by being, we share by our presence that God is in our lives.

I almost always have a smile on my face because the feeling of joy is always present and is asking to shine through me. Opportunities are always present to let others in on our secret, and the opportunities of volunteering an answer at an opportune moment or when asked always occur. God will bring those open to hearing the message into our lives at the appropriate moment. We must practice these principles in all areas of our lives.

When we walk the path to abundance, we live out the path in everything we do. It becomes second nature as time goes on, and we find it difficult to know otherwise.

The key is daily quiet time. Every day. Without fail.

If we live with daily quiet time, trusting in the wisdom of God, even if we find ourselves in situations that seem far from God, the Divine Wisdom will prevail and clear the paths in our lives. I found myself expressing myself in ways that were detrimental to my family, marriage, and career—let alone the feeling of the presence the Divine Wisdom in my life.

God led me to seek out a community practicing the twelve steps of Alcoholics Anonymous to combat many other practices in life, including depression and anxiety. I was relieved of the sadness that often overrode my joy, which was confusing to me to say the least. The prolonged exposure to the twelve steps led me to firming up the process that I have been writing about. Having such a program in my life clearly spelled out gives clarity to my points when I speak about the process, and it has been a joyful pathway for many years. The twelve steps spelled out, point by point, the path I had followed most of my life without realizing it. Since I had no knowledge of the path when I was in trouble, I floundered until the Divine Wisdom showed me the defined path that I have followed now for thirty years.

And the key, even when my behavior was way less than I desired, was that I never gave up on the quiet time in my life. Coincidence? I do not believe so. These events have been a gift from the Divine Wisdom, leading me to see the path I had been following without realizing the nature of the path. I can now share this path with others.

I can now see clearly that God has never let me down and has always been there to guide me—sometimes hitting me firmly over the head to catch my attention.

"Beauty is not who you are on the outside;
it is the wisdom and time you gave away
to save another struggling soul, like you."
Shannon L. Alder

Step 12. We are committed to continued exploration of these sacred dimensions in our lives. We will endeavor to pass these practices and purposes to others seeking joy and happiness and practice these principles in our lives.

Questions to Ponder

In your daily life, do you see opportunities where you can apply these principles and show others their wonder? Write down when such an opportunity appears—and write your response to that opportunity.

Does the daily quiet time or meditation time seem like too much to chew off by committing to it for life?

Write down your feelings, and then change the time-period to "daily prayer time for just today," and see how that time period seems. The AA saying—"One day at a time"—applies here. Just have a quiet time today. Write down if you can have a quiet time today.

Meditation

Oh, Divine Wisdom, I marvel, looking back on my life as I ponder these words, how your guidance has always been present in my life, gently or firmly, depending on the situation, speaking through my guides or mentors, and the hundreds of books you have led me to in my lifetime, leading me through fair weather and stormy weather. I bow gratefully and place my being in your presence, giving me respite even when the waves were seemingly overpowering. Your shadow over me and in me has led me to a place of peace, and I understand the path that you have led me through. I am grateful for this opportunity to share your presence with all who come this way. May we all find the peace and joy that you promise us, which is ours for the asking in this life.

Chapter 31

Twelve Steps to a Life of Peace, Joy, and Happiness

I have been describing each of the twelve steps and the process involved in each step, and this chapter is the twelve steps to a life of peace, joy, and happiness in a single listing. These steps are a slight modification of the original twelve steps of Alcoholics Anonymous, and they came to my thought process as a gift from my Divine Wisdom, one step at a time. We will continue to discuss the implications of the steps that will result in a life filled with joy and happiness until we pass into the next realm of life.

Step 1. We admitted we were powerless over our ego—that our lives were unmanageable and filled with unease and restlessness.

Step 2. We came to believe that a power greater than our egos could restore us to sanity.

Step 3. We made a decision to turn our will and our lives over to the care of God as we understood God.

Step 4. We made a fearless examination of what was preventing us from surrendering our lives over to the care of God as we understood God.

Step 5. We admitted to God, ourselves, and another person the nature of our fears, resentments, worries, anxieties, and grievances.

Step 6. We ask God to remove these barriers to a full and rich life—one filled with joy and happiness.

Step 7. We acknowledge both the light and dark elements of our nature as to who we are in the deeper reality of our being.

Step 8. We take responsibility for our choices that have unintended consequences, including creating pain for others and ourselves.

Step 9. We commit to a life of healing and transformation. Through our thoughts, words, and actions, we will demonstrate who we are in truth.

Step 10. We continue to examine our lives and pursue a spiritual solution by surrendering to God.

Step 11. We commit to using various forms of prayer and meditation to increase our conscious contact with

God, praying only for the knowledge of God's desires for us and our willingness to carry that out.

Step 12. We are committed to continued exploration of these sacred dimensions in our lives. We will endeavor to pass these practices and purposes to others seeking joy and happiness and practice these principles in our lives.

Chapter 32

Quiet Time

The seed that fell among the thorns,
These are the ones who have heard,
And as they go on their way they are choked
With worries and riches and pleasures of
this life,
And bring no fruit to maturity.
—Luke 8:14, NASB

Why do we need quiet time? That question has been asked repeatedly. Most do not want to take time out of their busy schedules and then wonder why that great feeling they had from some spiritual experience drifts off. They find themselves looking back and wondering what happened.

Jesus said, *"The seed that fell among the thorns, these are the ones who have heard, and as they go on their way they are choked with worries and riches and pleasures of this life, and bring no fruit to maturity"* (Luke 8:14).

For the majority of those who have had a momentary glimpse of the Divine, this is their story. We are surrounded by the inputs of the five senses: sight, hearing, smell, taste, touch. These are the data inputs into our minds, and they fill every waking moment of our lives. There is no way to stop these inputs, and they dominate all that we understand about life. Today's technology has multiplied the effects to the point where the din of information makes the mind race from waking until falling asleep exhausted.

However, we can learn to use the sixth sense, that sense of the unconsciousness—where other energies, different from the energies used by the five senses, dominate.

The Sixth Sense

We have often called the sixth sense our intuitive sense, and while that is true, it is the sense that operates outside our normal vibrational regime of the five senses. Our five senses are a tiny portion of the vibrational potential wherein we are immersed. The universe contains the extremely low vibrations of the big bang to the extremely high frequencies of the quantum world. In that God world, only pure energy exists. We sense a very narrow band of the universe, and the infinite bands of God extend beyond that of the universe. The sixth sense can be tuned to match a portion of the God energy that we are immersed in.

We need to tune in so they can guide us into the realm beyond the five senses.

The sixth sense has no boundaries, and it can be opened to where the Creator of the universe operates, which is beyond the five senses.

Many people ask why God does not appear to us to confirm the Creator's existence, and that cannot be denied. If that occurred, we would immediately claim to know exactly what God looks like in our narrow perceptual bands. We'd erect statues and all kinds of idolatry to say that is God—and no other.

As we innately understand, God has no form but all forms. To say that is God or this is God misses the whole point of God being the All In All. In a true sense, God does this all the time—in everything we can touch, see, feel, taste, or hear. Our minds cannot wrap themselves around the subtle shifts that occur in the cacophony of noise that bombards our senses.

Awareness

But even this is God, if we but have eyes to see. The sixth sense has a unique ability to become aware of the infinite universe beyond the five senses. All sentient beings of the universe employ this sense to become aware of the infinite beyond our physical capabilities. The capability to sense the great beyond is in all, and some are fortunate to understand that at a very early age, but most of us must hone that capability to be able to go beyond the five senses.

That honing of the sixth sense is the purpose of the quiet time efforts.

When we learn to listen with the sixth sense, the movement of the Divine within us becomes clear in our beings. Our inner lives become a song in conjunction with the Divine. I describe it as a subtle sense of awareness or an inner sense of joy, waiting to bubble to the surface of my life. Even if I find myself deviating from my mark by

Truth is not something outside to be discovered; it is something inside to be realized.

—Osho

becoming angry or worse, the absence of the awareness of the Divine Wisdom alerts me that I am in a danger zone. When I return to my internal awareness, that feeling of the Divine is always present.

Our five senses are constantly filled, and the purpose of quiet time is to still the receptors of the five senses and let the sixth sense roam the realm of the universe. Only then can we see the vision of joy and happiness that await us. The sixth sense is not limited by the physical world we live in, and it is free to explore the infinite realm of the Creator within each of us. We are made in the image of God and are not bound by our physicality. The sixth sense is connected directly to the infinite power of the Divine. The sixth sense is free to roam the universe, and it is free to create a life within us of joy, peace, and happiness.

For most of us, the sixth sense is buried and must be resurrected. That resurrection is conceived by what I am calling Quiet Time. It is critical to arrange an internal promise that we will continue a daily period of quiet time under all circumstances, in one form or another. Even if the day is extremely packed, five minutes can be found to breathe deeply and relax, with eyes closed, and put oneself into the cloud of unknowing that awaits us at all moments.

The Lifetime Sequence of Quiet Time

The exhilaration we find when starting daily quiet time is palpable, and we find no problems with carving out the allotted time—be it ten minutes or an hour. Life tends to get in the way, (as Jesus said, *"And as they go on their way they are choked with worries and riches and pleasures of this life"*) and we find ourselves missing a time here and there. Pretty soon, we realize that we have missed a week or more—and we wonder what happened. We buckle down and start afresh, really meaning to do it daily. We again find ourselves missing a day and then a week. This sequence will repeat itself until we quit—and look back wistfully at that exciting time when the possible touch of God seemed so real. That sequence has happened to countless people I have talked with.

Jesus said, *"Other seed fell on rocky soil, and as soon as it grew up, it withered away, because it had no moisture"* (Luke 8:6).

How do we nurture this initial excitement into flower? How do we supply the moisture?

That is the question we will now explore.

Maintaining Quiet Time

I have been committed to a daily quiet time for more than fifty-five years, but I did not call it quiet time until twenty years ago or so. I have used many, many forms of prayer, meditation, readings, and more (some not so quiet) during that time, but the most difficult effort was maintaining the effort over the years. Between helping raise seven children, a demanding job that usually took more than forty hours a week, traveling on business extensively (I was traveling parts of, or on full days, 210 days one year), leading or facilitating groups or being part of a group throughout that time, our lives were busy. Finding the time each day to sit quietly with God was critical to maintaining any semblance of sanity.

I have watched hundreds of people start off with an enthusiastic bang on a daily prayer time and then fizzle out, even when they had some support. I know of few who have maintained a consistent time over many years of prayer to reach God without a strong support system, especially when that prayer time aimed at finding joy, peace, and happiness over time was an explicit goal. My strong support system lasted more than twenty-five years, which left me with the inner strength when that ended to continue without failure to this day. I have once again found a support group, and we share our daily struggles in a study fashion.

A strong support system is a two-way path, taking the time to reach out to the support group and absorbing the strength of the group when needed. This means setting aside the time to do this on a consistent basis.

Some may say, "But I have so many things to do."

That is all the more reason to spend time to strengthen oneself and look at oneself in a manner so that we are not doing good things so we can be seen as good people. We must fulfill the opportunities God presents us in our daily journeys. The key to this level of understanding is seeing ourselves as facilitators of the physicality of God. We must let the works and words of God flow through us as a conduit of God's grace. God works primarily through humanity on this planet. Only humanity has the potential of an awareness of the Spirit. We are self-aware to the point that the subconscious world can be made manifest to conscious awareness.

All things that we see, from the smallest organism to the outer universe, speak of God, but only those species called to be fully sentient are capable of an awareness of this relationship. Because we have this innate awareness, we are capable of a conscious link with the All in All. We have the capability of forging this link in the world of the physical, and we may act as the Word of God if we turn our lives over to the care of God.

As Jesus did, and as Jesus promised, when asked about his miracles, *"Greater things than this shall you do"* (John 14:12.).

To understand how Jesus had 'no doubt', we but see: *"But Jesus Himself would often slip away to the wilderness and pray"* (Luke 5:16, NASB).

Jesus understood that he had to take the time to reach into the infinite byways and commune with the All in All. Jesus had crowds that desired healings, words of wisdom, and joy and peace. He *"would often slip away and pray."* We too can learn to slip away and pray.

Jesus and other great masters understood that they had to find the time to commune with the Divine Wisdom—no matter what was going on around them. They would always find the time to commune with their souls—the part that was a direct extension of God.

Jesus said, *"Greater things than this shall you do."* He implied that when you reach that level of confidence and awareness of the Divine Wisdom that Jesus had, you can *"hurl that mountain into the sea,"* and other wondrous things will occur.

Perhaps even more critical is understanding the implication of Jesus's words. We have the innate capability to do wondrous things if we believe without a doubt. Jesus did not doubt. The miracles will occur if we do not doubt we can do *"greater things than this."*

The key to these greater things is committing to quiet time and fusing ourselves into an awareness of our souls—the essence of who we are.

> ***"True power is within,***
> ***and it is available now."***
> ***Eckhart Tolle***

Questions to Ponder

How do you view taking the time to directly immerse yourself in God every day? Write down your thoughts on this.

How do you view taking the time to directly immerse yourself in God today? Write down your feeling about this question.

Do you see that every day is just yesterday's tomorrow? Do you see the mind adjustment required to change the daunting thought of 'every day' being only 'today'?

Meditation

Oh, Divine Wisdom, who eagerly waits for the invitation to bloom in my soul. I gratefully extend that invitation from my soul to your living presence to bring my soul to the awareness of who I am: the image of God. Fill my being with the awareness of the Holy Spirit so that my cry to the universe is a cry to the soul of the universe. My very nature cries out for this freedom. I know that my soul has this freedom, but I have blinded myself with the sounds and sights of the universe that I can sense. These are but a minute fraction of the glory that is mine to enjoy if I wish. I open up my being to welcome the Universal Being that has been waiting for my invitation all my life. I know deep in my heart that you have granted this to me in this instance—and in all the instances of my life—focusing on this now as the only now that exists.

I am free. I bow in gratitude for this freedom.

Chapter 33

Do Not Doubt

Seek first the kingdom of God
and all these things shall be added to you.
—Matthew 6:33, ESV

*A*bundance is the magical name that seems to
promise wealth, a beautiful or handsome spouse,
a great home, and no problems anywhere. All we need
do is concentrate and remain focused on these physical
dreams—and they will be ours just by wishing it so.

Not quite! All of those things are niceties by
themselves. Even if we have them all, they will
eventually prove to be empty boxes and sounding
gongs with no real meaning in the depth of our hearts.

True abundance follows the words of Jesus. *"Seek
first the kingdom of God—and all these things shall
be added to you"* (Matt. 6:33).

True abundance is a heart matter. True abundance
renders us peace, joy, and happiness. When that
happens, we will have sufficient internal presence to
understand that *"all these things were added to us."*

Indeed, true abundance leaves a bubbling in the mind. Just around the corner, God is playfully hidden among the clatter of life.

A life of abundance is ours for the gathering. What we are doing in our quiet time is placing ourselves in a space where we can begin the process of coming face to face with God in our lives since that is where God is present.

Jesus said, *"The kingdom of God comes not by observation. Neither shall they say 'Here it is' or 'There it is,' for you see, the kingdom of God is within you"* (Luke 17:21, American King James Version, English Revised Version).

We see that the problem is simple: if the kingdom of God lies within each of us, the key to unlocking all that Jesus said is in the ability to reach that *"kingdom of God that lies within."*

There is a second part to the issue. *"If you have faith and do not doubt, you... can say to the mountain 'Be taken up and thrown into the sea,' and it will happen"* (Matt. 21:21, NIV).

Do not doubt! We all were suspicious that there was a catch, and there it is: *"Do not doubt."* How can we not doubt? Our five senses are bombarded day and night with 'reality', and 'reality' states that there is no way for that mountain to be hurled into the sea!

We begin to see the necessity to withdraw from the bombardment of the five senses and to begin to cultivate the sixth sense. That sense that is open to the infinite variety of the world beyond the extremely limited world of the five senses. We rely on our five senses for almost everything. Even those who should know better do the same. Physicists rely on machines to measure tiny perturbations in the percentages of the energy levels of the universe, and they claim that unless they can see and touch that creative power we call God, they will not believe. It seems a bit two-faced in my opinion since they rely on machines and formulas to claim all they know, but they refuse to use their internal sixth sense to claim what is present in giant form for all to behold.

Perhaps it is a case of the "not-invented-here" syndrome, where many companies refuse to acknowledge anything outside their own thought processes can be true—even if it causes them grief to not acknowledge what is evident to all. Those refusing to expand their internal capabilities beyond their five senses to include their sixth sense are more than willing to fill their minds with words and wisdom of those who only see with the five senses.

Perhaps the greatest giant of them all, Albert Einstein, understood this only too well. He said, *"Science without religion is lame; religion without science is blind."* Einstein understood the two sides of the controversy, and he would be appalled to see science and religion at war today. Both sides claim the other side is wrong.

In quiet time, we tune ourselves to the infinite world beyond the five senses and train ourselves to reach into the *"kingdom of God that lies within."* Like any sense, the sixth sense must be exercised and used. As the exercising continues, it will be sharpened to allow us to see things that have always been there. A paleontologist can spot rocks in the field that are bones of long dead creatures, while to the rest of us all we see is rocks and more rocks.

The Kingdom of God Within

This puzzling statement by Jesus has been modified by various translators, ignored by most (especially when combined with the power of the words of Jesus that spoke of the strength of what lies within), and downplayed as another example of exaggeration by Jesus that should not be taken literally. After all, did not Jesus undergo torture and death? How could the kingdom of God lie within?

Perhaps Jesus meant what he said. After all, it is spoken of in several contexts, and Jesus pointed at it in more than one gospel.

Let us look at that unusual statement. What could Jesus have been talking about when replying to the Pharisees?

> *Let us make humanity in our image, according to our likeness—so God created humanity in God's own image, in God's own image God created them, male and female God created them.*
> *—Genesis 1:27, NIV*

Jesus was apparently talking about the soul—that branch of God that never dies and is the basis of who we are in truth. The soul certainly fits the criteria that Jesus spoke of in his statement: it lies in our hearts of hearts, it has the potential of the kingdom of God since it is made in the image of God (Genesis), and having been made in the image of the Creator of the universe, it certainly would have the ability to transcend the physical laws of the universe to obey the command of the Creator.

Our Sixth Sense

I believe this is one of the most misunderstood and misbelieved phrases in the Bible. Even those who have a wide range of belief and understanding express total misbelief at this quote. "Certainly not me! Look at me—do I look like God?"

God has told me that when the Almighty Wisdom looks at you, he is amazed that you do not see that glorious picture, blazing with the knowledge and wisdom of God that shines forth from your soul, radiating from your body. I, occasionally, have been given the gift of seeing God in the faces of those I see, and I am almost blinded by what I see.

Why don't we see the glory of God when we look into a mirror? We see only the infinitely small spectrum of the universe—the portion used by the five senses to guide us in the world of physicality that we call home.

God sees the *"the kingdom of God that lies within"* in each one of us. The kingdom is totally dazzling if we but have eyes to see. That is the purpose of the quiet time. The sixth sense reigns supreme if we learn to use it as much as our other senses.

The sixth sense is tuned to behold where the infinite power of the universe resides. If we so wish, we can *"hurl that mountain into the sea."*

The sixth sense sees infinitely more than the other five senses combined. The tiny spectrum our five senses use allow us to function well in the physical world, but the five senses portray only a small portion of the information that surrounds us. Our minds, which operate only from a point that emanates from our past experiences, receive what information passes unto us from our five senses. They modify and decode the incoming information in ways that support our internal beliefs about the world we live in.

The world we think we live in is presented to us by our egos. The ego has us perceive all kinds of false things about our world, including the false notion that the world we perceive is the only true world. It attempts to drown any possibility that *"greater things than this"* are possible within the physical world.

The ego constantly says, "What I perceive is all that is—and what I perceive is the truth."

Another person, with the same data input from the five senses but a different background of experiences—perceives a totally different chain of events and believes that his or her perception of the event is the truth.

The truth of the world exists on so many different levels that no one but a master (such as Jesus or the Buddha) could perceive the truth of a given event. The true purpose of quiet time is to allow us to move into the world beyond that shown to us by the five senses and the ego. We arrive at the threshold of the infinite—where greater things than this are possible. We can state to that mountain, *"Hurl yourself into the sea,"* and it will be done.

> **"I have so much to do**
> **That I spend the first three hours in prayer."**
> **Martin Luther**

Questions to Ponder

Does it seem possible that all of your fears and doubts can be removed? Write down your gut feelings about that possibility.

Is it worth the effort to remove all fears and doubts from your mind every day?

Write down your feelings about accomplishing the goal of removing your fears and doubts from your mind. How much time you believe you would be willing to spend each day to accomplish that goal?

Meditation

Eternal Wisdom, I bow in gratitude for opening up the possibilities of shifting my perception of the world to include the wider perception of infinity that exists in my universe and beyond. That infinite power and possibilities are ours for the asking—if only I ask. I quiet the five senses I have used from childhood, and I dare to begin the process of strengthening my sixth sense, which is so much vaster than what the other five senses can perceive. I commit to training this sixth sense to perceive the world of infinity. I can begin to perceive your presence and gain that sense of wonder that is the core of my sixth sense. I understand that this process takes time and effort, and I commit myself to a daily time spent learning and deepening my sense of oneness with you. I will follow where you lead me, knowing that I will become sensitive to your words to me if I let go of my fears.

Chapter 34

Quiet Time: Time, Place

The main lesson about prayer is just this:
Do it! Do it! Do it! You want to be taught to
pray?
My answer is: Pray.
—John Laidlaw

When we think of quiet time or meditation, probably the first thing that comes to mind is someone sitting on the floor with legs crossed at the thighs, sitting upright with hands on knees and thumb and finger touching, eyes closed, and oblivious to the world.

In sixty years of daily quiet time, meditation, and prayer time, I have never sat on the floor like that. First of all, my knees would not take that kind of stretch. I have found it extremely uncomfortable to even sit on the floor, and anything uncomfortable takes me far from the space I want to be when working on my sixth sense.

In this discussion, I will be discussing the time and place of quiet time, using many sources I have read to draw inspiration. I mostly base it on more than sixty years of daily quiet time. Later we will discuss the *what* of quiet time.

My Experience

In the beginning, after I was in college and was on my own (about 1958), I had no name for quiet time. It was my daily prayer time. Like many Roman Catholics, I began with the daily Rosary, a rhythmic saying of five sets of ten Hail Mary prayers and associated prayers I had learned with my family while growing up. The daily Rosary was part of the fabric of our Roman Catholic family, stretching back into the 1930s. This took about twelve minutes. I also found the time to go to Mass once or twice a week besides Sunday. I found comfort in this, even in college, and since I went to a Catholic university (University of Dayton), no one found it strange to see me in the chapel. I continued this practice when I started my first job. There always seemed to be a Catholic church within a short driving distance that had a Mass around noon. I was using various means to talk to my God (I had not learned how to listen to God at that time) even before my experience in 1967.

In 1965, I became part of a group that met every week. Part of the practice was to talk briefly about our daily prayer time, as well as action, and it became self-supported with these weekly meetings. These meetings gave me the ongoing support I needed, and I rarely missed the meetings. I felt that I needed support as our family grew and the needs of my career grew, making it more difficult to find the time to spend talking with God. These meetings continued for more than twenty years and firmly cemented the concept and necessity of daily prayer time in my psyche.

After my experience with God in December 1967, my whole attitude with quiet time changed. My time with God, my Eternal Wisdom, became a two-way conversation. I would talk to God, and God would answer in feelings, words read, or words spoken to me. My decisions became very clear. The Eternal Wisdom would speak to me through others, most often through my wife or something I read.

This went on for years, moving around different methodologies and being led to different experiences that would increase my awareness of the presence of God in my daily life. My times and places for these moments of quiet time over the six decades changed constantly, depending on free time or family and career commitments. The principle behind the process is not what or how one finds the time; it is the relevance and commitment of the time spent each and every day.

Finding the Time

Finding the time to talk with God is perhaps the most difficult part of the commitment. Eventually, I needed thirty minutes or more each day. Now that I have more time, I spend an hour or more, much to my surprise. I used many references to fit the time into my schedule. The most common time was lunch. I would pack a lunch each morning (another sneaky time to find five minutes or so to dedicate the day to God), sit in the car, eat my lunch, read, and discuss my life with my Eternal One. If possible, I would head to a church. Even if no one were present, I'd sit on the altar steps, have a close conversation, wait for an answer, (a thought or a feeling) and move on.

Another time that many of us have is traveling to and from the office. That time can be spent listening to the voice of God that surrounds us at all times. Short, repetitive prayers are to be used so that proper attention is paid to the task of driving. Of course, if you use public transportation, it is easier to zone out and place oneself in the presence of the Divine. On public transportation, especially at rush hour, seeing the presence of the Eternal One in each person we are with is an added benefit, especially in those who seem irritable, sad, or pushy.

Rising early or just before bedtime are other useful times. I have used both methods when the day was full. It is a good practice upon rising to give thanks to God for another day to see the Eternal One in all things around me—even in a dirty diaper if that is where life is. That life you see and touch is one of greatest miracles of all.

It is always possible to find time for this daily effort. The problem is devoting that period to having conversations with God and not finding something else to fill the time, such as watching the news or a sports event on TV or just mind-filling things like a television show or book. Take the time to squirrel oneself away for the mind-expanding event of joining with the Eternal Wisdom for a visit.

Sacred Space

One of the best ways to have a place that draws you into the sacred zone is to set up a sacred space in the home or to have a "traveling sacred space." I have

Prayer is exhaling the spirit of man and inhaling the Spirit of God.
—Edwin Keith

used both approaches, especially when traveling for business. One of the better ways at home is to have a corner of a room with a small table and a picture or a statue, and a candle to set the tone. I went through many a votive candle and many smaller or larger candles over the years. I traveled with a small candle and a cloth, and I would clear an area and spread the sacred cloth over the desk in the hotel room, light the candle, and do whatever I had in mind. Eastern traditions strongly urge a sacred space be kept in the home; growing up in the forties and fifties, my parents kept such a space in our living room.

My current sacred space is in the living room. I am blessed with a view of the foothills of the mountains to the east. On a clear day, I can see for about thirty miles, and when it snows, the beauty is breathtaking. We are surrounded by forests, but living on top of the five hundred-foot hill and with some judicious clearing, our view sweeps across the countryside in a panorama that always lifts my soul. I often use a candle to infuse that space, and when it is late at night or early in the morning, the magic fills that space. It is easy to put myself into communion with the Divine Wisdom.

There is no correct position for quiet time. I try to sit in a comfortable position on a comfortable chair or the couch. I breathe easily and deeply to clear my mind and body, and I keep my back straight. The lotus position—with legs crossed and locked, back straight and hands on knees—was developed to provide a position of strength and openness. It allows open breathing and open spirit without having to pay attention to the body. I have never used that position, but I do try to keep my upper body open and relaxed as possible—even when lying down.

I was taught to keep my spine erect but not stiff by sitting comfortably but erect in a chair. I place my open hand on top of my head. With slight pressure, I pull my head straight up, which slightly lengthens my spine. When I feel a firming of my spine and head, I go into quiet time and let myself sink into the Holy Spirit.

When our children were growing up, the house was always in an uproar. I would take a bedroom that had been emptied (our children were born over a seventeen-year period) and set up the sacred space in a corner. I was ready to move it when they all came home. When the family descends in large groups (a family reunion including cousins can reach fifty), that space is not possible. Joining with the Divine Wisdom becomes part of the blessed chaos going on in that moment.

God speaks to us in many ways and in many forms. It is still surprising when I sense the Divine Spirit in the middle of a family get-together. I step back from the music, laughing, good food, and loving attention and let the Divine Wisdom fill my soul. Joy flows around and in me for some time. That is quiet time in the essence.

"God dwells where we let God in."
Menachem Mendel

Questions to Ponder

Look at the schedule of your life. Do you find time in that schedule where a program could be missed? Would a change here or there free fifteen minutes of your day to spend with your Divine Wisdom? Write it down to remind yourself that this scheme will work.

A week later, look at your results. How did you do with finding the time for quiet time? Write this down. Adjust your schedule as necessary.

For several weeks, write down how you managed to fit the quiet time into your day. Adjust as required to find the time.

Meditation

Divine Spirit, you fill my life daily with the essence of your being. My problem has always been quieting the five senses so I can hear and feel your presence in the wider spectrum of the sixth sense—even when the five senses are filled with activity. You have given me the essence of quiet time to hone the sixth sense so it is as active as my five ordinary senses. I cannot express enough gratitude for these lessons you have given me in learning to see your presence in all things. I live in a seemingly lonely atmosphere, and I am especially grateful for learning to sense your active presence at all times—even when alone or when surrounded by many. You grant me the time and space needed if I wish, and this time spent in conscious awareness talking and listening to you over the years has granted me the wisdom and knowledge of your being in ways that cannot be put into words. They are expressed in feelings and a sense of awareness.

I rest myself into your being and content myself with the knowledge that all is indeed well—and that all will be well in the future.

Chapter 35

Quiet Time: The How

Knock, and God will open the door.
Vanish, and God will make you shine like
the sun.
Fall, and God will raise you to the heavens.
Become nothing,
And God will turn you into everything.
—Rumi

The Tools of Prayer

We are talking here about the tools of prayer. Prayer itself is not a thing one does; it is a state of being in a relationship with the Great Unknown. We can sense that void, but we have no idea what it means. These various tools provide a means to reach that void. We join more personally with that unknown to become more fully who we really are—beings made in the image of the Divine Wisdom.

When we first start the daily practice, the world seems full of things to meditate on or to use as tools for quiet time. As time goes by, it can become a challenge to find material that is fresh and challenging. The purpose of prayer is to build a relationship. Those of us who have successfully survived a long relationship understand the necessity of maintaining freshness in that relationship, and prayer is no different. Repeating the same approach too many times can provide a death knoll to any relationship, prayer included.

I have used many techniques over the years, and I still find that reading a spiritual book is one of the best lead-ins to time with the Divine Wisdom. God speaks to us in many ways, and I will present a few of the possible ways. I am sure there are many ways to hear the Divine Whisper that I do not know. I am always finding wonderful new ways.

The Rosary was an ancient prayer form developed in early Christianity for those who could not read, which was the vast majority of people. It is still popular in the Roman Catholic Church, especially among the elderly. Simple prayers like this (simplicity is one of keys to conversing with the Divine Wisdom) can fill the day in a peaceful manner. My birth family, like many Catholic families in the 1940s, said a daily Rosary together. I used that prayer form for more than forty years— sometimes with months or years in between use.

I used the Book of Hours for thirty years; the extensive prayer form used by the Roman Catholic clergy and others, consisting of various psalms,

The moment God is figured out with nice neat lines and definitions, we are no longer dealing with God.
—Rob Bell

biblical and ancient holy readings, and other prayers set at various times of the day, such as Morning Prayer, Evening Prayer, Matins (look it up), and other times. The prayers were set in a combination of seasonal and four-week cycles. They vary according to the season (Advent, Christmas, Lent, Easter, and ordinary time). I found the prayers helpful and soothing, especially when I questioned what was going on in my life.

There is something about using a form of prayer that is used by millions to gather strength when needed and to feel part of a worldwide layer of God on this planet that is understood by many. I would rarely say all of the prayers. I usually focused on morning and evening prayers.

I am an avid reader and much prefer reading to watching television. I am a searcher for truth in the world. I bought books—used when I could—by theologians and spiritual writers. The works of the Second Vatican Council gave many of us in the Catholic Church great hope. I read anything that could further my thirst for knowledge and understanding in spirituality and science. I believe strongly that for one (spirituality or science) to be true, then the other (science or spirituality) must say something similar, using different words but the same meaning. Science is working out the truth of the universe in a physical manner. My studies of physics, both the very, very large and the very, very small—the cosmos and quantum physics—have allowed me to glimpse God in entirely new ways. God is certainly greater than our universe; but the universe is an expression of God, just as we humans are an expression of God, as it says in Genesis 1.

This has been my journey. Today, I use short meditations, walks in the garden for my health, gardening, the art form of bonsai (miniature trees), writing, and reading.

Reading Quiet Time

Quiet time using spiritual reading is not the same as spiritual reading for knowledge—even though spiritual reading for knowledge can become a time of quiet time. Quiet time, in its essence, is a time for communion with the Spirit of Wisdom. I use words from a book to act as a guide into the time for Communion. One of the most time-tested methods is randomly opening a holy book (and any spiritual book can be a holy book) and reading the first thing your eyes settle on. Close the book and ponder what you just read. This works well for many. I have rarely used this approach since it generally works best with books where you know the content well.

I often use books as the source of my quiet time, usually reading relatively slowly a book by an author I trust. When something strikes me, I stop and reread the paragraph or phrase and let it sink into my spirit. The pause needs only be a few seconds, but it often leads to letting the feelings and thoughts flow through me.

A surprising amount of time can pass before I resume reading. I have used the Conversations with God series by Neale Donald Walsch for more than fifteen years. I read one section or paragraph, sometimes even less, stop, and meditate on that portion.

A book does not have to be a spiritual book to have spiritual meaning. I am a bit of a science nut, and I often read books on quantum physics. I find profound insights mentioned in those books about the nature of the universe and use them to explore what it says about the nature of God and myself.

Some of the other better-known authors I use are Richard Rohr, Teilhard de Chardin, Deepak Chopra, Debbie Ford, Diarmuid O'Murchu, Dr. Wayne Dyer, Maryanne Williamson, the Dalai Lama, and Richard Bach. This is only a small sampling of the authors I have read over the years, and books by these and so many other wonderful authors await discovery. I have read hundreds of spiritual books, and I have at least six open on my iPad—plus four hardback books with bookmarks on the coffee table.

Walking Quiet Time

Anytime we take the time to walk—for exercise, joy of movement, or to see the sights—is a time to join oneself with the Divine. One way that is exquisite is mentioned in *The Divine Milieu* by Teilhard de Chardin is called the "Luminous World."

In order to discover and frequently exercise your new eyes to discern the fire or luminosity within things, start small. Choose one living thing, such as a flower, a bug, a pet, or a baby, and with your imagination picture a kind of glow or luminousness surrounding and penetrating the object of your contemplation. Stay with it for a few minutes, focusing not on the external beauty or complexity of the object but upon the glow surrounding and penetrating it, as if that were its source of life and existence.

Once you learn to do this, the glow or luminosity will develop a life of its own. Then you can move to another object of contemplation to witness its glowing luminosity.

From time to time, say a word of thanks to this benevolent God who is constantly revealing God's form to you everywhere in creation. (Louis M. Savary, Teilhard de Chardin, The Divine Milieu Explained)

God is everywhere, in everything, waiting for us to open our eyes and see the glory that is always there. The glory of God is revealed in the simple things.

Watching Quiet Time

I learned a useful technique from the work of Gurdjieff and Ouspensky. Self-observation is similar to the approaches taught in the mastermind groups. It is by recognizing that we can learn to step back mentally and observe the constant stream of thoughts that occur from the various sources in our minds, which are usually from the more negative side of our egos. When we learn to do that, and it is not difficult since the din of the thought stream is so loud, we see that most thoughts have nothing to do with what is going on in the perceived world.

We have random thoughts, most often of a negative variety, about others or events where we felt wronged in some way. When we learn self-observation, we discover how judgmental we are about so many things—and how totally useless this process really is. It only creates negative images and feeds our negative perceptions of the world.

When we learn to move into the position of self-observation, we will be amazed at our thoughts. We will wonder where in the world they came from since they appear to be so foreign to what we like to think we think. It is as if we have another person sitting just out of view, talking constantly about everything under the sun, criticizing, and judging everything. They aim to prove that we are superior to all else around us.

It is from this center of being that self-observation brings us that we can move into more conscious conduct—not always dwelling on past events or future catastrophes. We can live in the most blessed event of all: the now. The more we can observe ourselves and correct or slow down the chatter, the more we will be able to see the glory of God in this life we are living. It is from this center that we can move into the essence of quiet time, that stillness in life, that silence between thoughts, which will be present. We can begin the process of hearing God speaking in our thoughts and feelings.

The first layer is the most important, and it is easy to learn the technique with a little effort. It is a wonderful way to still the mind, the most difficult task in quiet time.

This technique leads naturally into the flow of being awake, the state of life where we live only in the present moment. Eckhart Tolle discusses this in *The Power of Now.*

> *"When one is awake, every moment is alive. We not only become conscious of the stream of thought, we find that, that stream dwindles to a mere background noise, and we see the glorious brightness of the present moment, the only moment where God exists. The world will be brighter because we focus on this moment, any time we can devote our full attention to the now, our senses are all tuned to this moment and life becomes*

much more exciting, and the quiet time becomes the only moment that there is, which is a discovery of one of the great truths of our lives, that only this moment is real."

Breathing Quiet Time

Observing the breath is an excellent way to move from the chaotic world into a single focus. While the mind seems to be filled with many streams of thought, a single stream rapidly switches from one topic to another. We feel like we are running in parallel paths. When you give the mind a single focus, in this case the breath, it suppresses the running stream of thought. The principle is simple: just watch your breath, in and out. Do not attempt to control your breath. Just let your body breathe naturally.

Breath control is possible, and many books have advocated it, but it can be dangerous unless under the guidance of a master. Once we control our breathing, unless under strict control, we can break the automatic breathing response of the body and do damage to ourselves. There is no danger in just watching our breathing and marveling at the way life-giving oxygen is fed to the body in just the proper amounts.

As you learn to relax the body and move more deeply into quiet time, you will see your breathing slow down, deepen, and smooth out. Focus on your breathing, let your thought pattern broaden slightly, and feel the warmth of God enveloping you. Follow that gentle pull while watching your breath—unless you are pulled into the flow of God. If so, the breath will take care of itself.

In book 3 of Conversations with God, Neale Donald Walsch said,

> *"God said: Breathe. That is another tool. Breathe long and deep. Breathe slowly and gently. Breathe in the soft, sweet nothingness of life, so full of energy, so full of love. It is God's love you are breathing. Breathe deeply, and you can feel it. Breathe very, very deeply, and the love will make you cry.*
>
> *For joy.*
>
> *For you have met your God, and your God has introduced you to your soul."*

Song Quiet Time

Any of the methods discussed previously will be enhanced if music is included. If the atmosphere is set properly, an appropriate song or musical background can be used as a focal point to stop the chatter of the mind. I played the guitar for many years—until a finger injury prevented me from playing—and I would play and sing melodies that spun me into quiet time. I would often continue playing and let my mind merge with the great source.

It can be any kind of music, depending on your mood. If my mood were agitated, I could play or listen to a rousing Dixieland tune that would bring me to joy. I usually slow it down to gentle background sound or even just strum the guitar for a rhythmic background. A waterfall effect can soothe the mind and soul.

Deepak Chopra uses a gentle flowing sound to enhance the effect of his meditation streams. These background sounds are available by themselves to use as you wish and can be programmed on the computer for any length as desired.

Nature can provide natural melodies and soothing sounds. Sitting under a tree and listening to the breeze, sitting by a fountain or waterfall, or sitting by a stream can do wonders for the soul. It can lead to being at peace with yourself and the world.

Above all, we are searching for ways to lead us into the period of no time—when all else vanishes except for the place beyond what we see. And if it does not, it is all right. These moments of no time can be rare, but they will come when you are ready.

> *Your sacred space is where*
> *You can find yourself*
> *Over and over again.*
> *—Joseph Campbell*

Questions to Ponder

In a period of quiet time, how do you find your feelings and emotions? Do they settle down and relax? Do you find yourself wishing for more time or less? Search your feelings about why you feel in this way.

Write down your thoughts.

Meditation

My Divine Wisdom, I am grateful for leading me to find ways to still my runaway mind, still my agitation, and let me find a level of peace—no matter what is going on in my mind. I know that I can always find refuge from the storms of life by entering into the space where I can encounter the Holy Spirit within. Jesus said, "The kingdom of God is within." The spirit of peace that I am always searching for is always within me, waiting to be acknowledged and asked to become an active part of my conscious presence. That simple request will always be answered, and my daily practice keeps it close to my awareness. It is easy to turn to when a storm is nigh. I am grateful for the gift of quiet time in my life. It has allowed me to become more centered in my thoughts and actions.

Chapter 36

Quiet Time— Meditation

Meditation is a way for nourishing
And blossoming the divinity within you.
—Amit Ray

I will be speaking here of prayerful meditation. Meditation sort of snuck into Western awareness to reduce stress and other clinical problems. Meditation certainly works in these areas, but the original source of meditational practices came out of the Eastern society, especially India. For thousands of years, meditation practices were used to commune with the spirit and beyond.

The Trappist monk Thomas Merton wrote about fifty books, most of which attempted to show the power of Eastern practices of meditation. What is usually meant by meditation is to quiet one's thoughts to the point of silence for a length of time, often for thirty minutes or more.

I envy (I think) those who can do that. I can rarely shut my mind down, and I have a sneaking hunch that many who claim to do so find a stray thought or a hundred stray thoughts sneaking by. The purpose of self-observation, mantras, and breathing exercises is to occupy the mind and turn off the chatter. The mind is a receiver of information, and all have agreed that there is an overload of information in today's world. No previous generation has so much information available, pouring out of televisions, the Internet, radios, and books.

Once upon a time, when the source of information that was external to the mind came from another person and/or the environment or books, it was easier to reduce the stream of thoughts to silence. Even then, the ego, an ingenious source used to understand the physical world and manage the environment, became afraid it would lose power. It filled the mind with suggestions and random thoughts. We often find ourselves revisiting past events and saying, "If only this or that had been different." But, the past is set and cannot be changed.

Many of the tools I wrote about before can be utilized to control the mind when entering quiet time. Meditation, as it is usually understood, requires a quieting of the mind, sometimes with the aid of a mantra (a short simple saying) repeated over and over again. It usually follows a short reading or other source of thought that can be focused on with the second or third tier of the thinking web we employ. The reading should be performed with thoughtfulness and used to evoke a feeling or insight into a higher level of thinking than is used for day-to-day thoughts. There are many resources for meditation available in books and over the Internet.

The general process of meditation, as taught by most masters, is to settle in a comfortable position, in a chair, on the floor, or on a pillow. The position must be comfortable. The best type of position is one where you can be lost in the wonders of the universe (contemplation) without danger of falling over. The position should permit the blood to flow to the arms, legs, and feet without restriction. The position should be open to the universe and firm (but not rigid). The hands are open in your lap or on your knees and relaxed. If it makes you feel better, touch the thumb and forefinger together gently, but this is not necessary. In fact, none of it is necessary, but many have found it useful.

The purpose of meditation is to put oneself into a state of mind that is open to the Voice of God—if that is your gift at the moment. The term Voice of God usually means a feeling of bliss or happiness beyond understanding. You are aware of the God that lies

Work is not always required. There is such a thing as sacred idleness.
—George MacDonald

within, that kingdom of God that you have within and without you at all times.

God is not out there. Jesus said, *"The kingdom of God is not coming with signs to be observed. Nor will they say 'Look, here it is!' For behold, the kingdom of God is within"* (Luke 17:20–21, Revised English Version). The kingdom of God is not somewhere else. It is but in your very being, it *is* your very being, and it can be reached by a single thought.

The purpose of meditation is to reach that state where the kingdom of God is available to your mind— that bridge between the seemingly three-dimensional world that fills our daily lives (the ego) and the kingdom of God, our soul. This state comes at the beckoning of the Immortal Wisdom. All we can do is try to clear our minds of the garbage that seems to fill most of our thoughts. If the moment is appropriate for our path to this sojourn, a two-way direct conversation with the Eternal Wisdom can occur. It will usually be a lifting up of the spirit. Saint Paul said, *"I know a man in Christ who fourteen years ago, (whether in the body I do not know or out of the body I do not know—God knows) such a one was caught up to the third heaven"* (2 Corinthians 12:2, NIV). These moments are available for all since this "third heaven" is identical to "the kingdom of God that lies within."

Paul never heard Jesus preach, and he was probably unaware of these significant words spoken decades earlier. The gospels were not written until after Paul had transitioned. Paul was assuredly speaking of his own experiences, and apparently it was a rare

occurrence even for him. I had the experience once—
on Saturday, December 2, 1967—and remember it well.

Even if that level of direct experience of the kingdom
of God is rare, a connection with the *"kingdom that
lies within"* is not rare. It is possible to hold daily
conversations with God— both talking to and receiving
responses on a consistent basis. Once you have found
the path to reach to this level—connecting on this
basis and expecting and receiving answers—comfort
and guidance can be part of your life.

I am not worthy.

I am not worthy. This is a common response by most
major religions when asked about how to seek the
counsel of God. This advice is the advice of a group
setting themselves up over others to avoid serious
questions that are difficult to answer. They are
demanding control of others.

When asked about a conversation with God, some
people say, "You are not meant to know." They are
saying that you are not worthy of God. Only they are
worthy of telling you how to live, what not to do, what
to eat, and what to study. They want to control your
life as a child, all of your life, and will not permit you
to become an adult made *"in the image and likeness of
God."* However, you *are* worthy of seeing God as part
of the *"kingdom of God that lies within."*

Genesis starts off with the creation stories. *"God created humanity in God's own image, in the image of God, God created them; male and female God created them"* (Genesis 1:27, NIV).

God is beyond infinity, encompassing all that we know and so much more that we have not even guessed at yet. We are made in God's image, the image of the Divine Wisdom Herself. Anyone who has studied mathematics knows that any subset of infinity is also infinity. Mathematics also states that when something is a mirror image of another, they are equal to each other by default. That is if a=b, then a and b are the same. Are we equal to God in all things?

Jesus said, *"Greater things than this shall you do."*

I am not saying that we are equal to God in all ways—even though we are certainly capable of being as powerful as Jesus ("greater things than this shall you do") in the words of Jesus. Certainly we are worthy of being closer to God in all things. By the Word of God, we are the image of the Divine Wisdom, capable of anything we can imagine—if we move into a field of oneness between the mind and soul. Jesus's power, from which emanated his ability to heal, or 'to send mountains into the sea' if he wished, is ours as Jesus said. Having said that, Jesus' ability to state God's presence and love, the Christ presence, was Jesus' gift alone, as the living reality of the Christ, the son of God revealed at that moment.

The Purpose of Life

This movement into oneness of the mind and soul is the purpose of quiet time—and the goal of meditation of all types. The Conversation with God series states the purpose of life in the most succinct way I have ever seen: *"The purpose of life is to recreate yourself anew in the next grandest version of the grandest vision you ever held about who you are."* This statement is breathtaking. I have found that as I recreate myself in the next grandest vision, I am soon granted a new 'grandest vision' to recreate myself again. This increasing vision never ends.

We have all had a vision of ourselves that is much loftier than the one we seem to be living. Most of time, we are lost to that vision in the throes of everyday life. We get caught up with the next best thing or our jobs or finding money for the family. When we remember something we said we would do that seemed like such a great and lofty idea at the time, it is lost in the rush of life. Maybe it is time to step back and look at that idea again—and move to see what can be done to accomplish it.

A critical part of that process is aligning yourself with the purpose of that goal and seeing if that goal is part of the greatest vision you have for yourself. If it seems to be, perhaps now is the time. Meditation and quiet time need be a major part of that focus. The new version of you will not be a flash in the pan but a step to ease the pain that is so prevalent in the world today.

For I was hungry, and you gave me something to eat, I was thirsty and you gave me something to drink; I was a stranger and you invited me in, naked and you clothed me, I was sick and you visited me; I was in prison and you came to me. (Mathew 25:35-36, NIV)

Meditation Sources

Many meditation methods will lead directly into the silence of the soul, the goal of meditation. I especially like the recent twenty-minute meditation recordings of Deepak Chopra and Oprah, in units of twenty-two meditations on a topic.

If you wish to establish a daily routine of prayer and mind shift, I recommend strongly *A Course In Miracles*, which is a year-long set of meditation practices meant to bring a person to a closer relationship with the Divine Wisdom. I have been through the course several times, and I find it very useful for furthering my spiritual goals in life.

In 2015, a powerful version by James Twyman (jamestwyman.tv) was released. James provides a sung introduction, a reading of the daily lesson with emphasis on meaning, and a two-minute reflection that fills in the meaning. If I cannot find time early in the day to listen, I am not afraid to skip a day and pick up where I left off the next day.

A Trappist monk, Thomas Keating, introduced the 'centering prayer' that many have found profoundly helpful. Centering prayer was developed from *The Cloud of Unknowing,* a fourteenth-century Christian mystical manual of the inner life. A short passage is read from a spiritual book, usually only a sentence or two, and then you sit quietly and let your mind absorb the message, using your sacred word to move from thoughts that arise. The recommended way to handle the chaotic stream of thoughts from the ego is to just let the thought float by and not let it catch your attention. When you find yourself caught in a thought, just let it go and repeat your sacred word. The thought will just drift away and become a nonentity in the quieting process. This process may take some time to learn because it is destroying the death grip that the ego has on our consciousness. It permits the mind to reach beyond the ego in new ways. A new book by Cynthia Bourgeault, is extremely helpful: *"the Heart of Centering Prayer"* (2017). I have found Centering Prayer similar to what Eckhart Tolle advocates to work only in the 'now'.

A spiritual teacher by the name of Osho has many profound forms and topics that have taught thousands how to meditate. He has more than twenty books that are devoted to bringing readers into a more perfect alignment with the soul.

There are many more wonderful authors and leaders of meditation practices, and I could write a whole book and not cover them all. The Internet is a good place to find teachers, and if you are serious, then start looking.

An awake heart is like a sky that pours light.
—Hafez

Questions to Ponder

Find a time when you have an hour or so when you can be alone with your thoughts and try one of these techniques. Write down your feelings about each approach. Do not do more than two in any one session.

Pick the top two or three approaches from your initial efforts. Spend one week doing just one, each day if possible, at any chosen time of day. Write down your feelings each day.

Pick your best method and use it until it feels stale. Then pick another method.

Meditation

Holy Wisdom, I am filled with love for the joy that you have brought into my life through prayer, quiet time, meditation, and contemplation. You have shown me—even through struggles and pain—that consistently returning to the Source will provide me with the strength and patience to find the way to joy and happiness. It may take much time, but I am filled with gratitude for my life. This has led to much deep discovery into the eternal realm that fills and surrounds us at all times—even when we are blinded to its existence. I ask that all be open to receiving this gift of joy, which is available to all. Your gift is breathtaking, beyond all measure, taking the soul and our spirit to dwell among the saints and angels of the life that surrounds us, indwells in us, and fills the universe.

Chapter 37

Contemplation

Muddy water, let stand, becomes clear.
—Lao Tzu

*T*he central theme of all quiet time and meditation is that unexpected moment when we find ourselves in the very presence of the universe, our Eternal Wisdom. Contemplation, in the context spoken here, is not something one does. It is a gift that occurs in an unguarded moment. It is that moment when you first see a newborn, and your breath catches, and your mind goes blank with the wonder of it all. Everyone has had moments when beauty and wonder catch him or her off guard. The breath catches, and time seems to stand still. Sometimes a sunset, a leaf, a sudden view, the moment when you realize that you want to spend your life with a certain someone can make time vanish. Everything seems suspended in nothingness. This is living as one "poor in spirit", and indeed, one is living in the "kingdom of heaven". (See Matthew 5:3)

Contemplation in this sense is a gift from the universe, the brush with eternity that makes life worth living. As soon as someone realizes he or she is in this timeless moment, the real world steps in— and that space is gone. The most frustrating part of contemplation is being in that state for only as long as one is not aware of being in that state. When it occurs, it is only a period of statelessness, a blank opening into eternity. Nothing else matters, and nothing else is present. It is a suspension of all that is, including time itself.

Contemplation, as I speak of it here, is that mystical place of nothing where only an awareness of being is present. It is a state of bliss. Pain ceases, the world itself ceases, and all else ceases to be part of awareness. This state is not a state we can figure out how to obtain; and is gifted to us from a power within and without. We become one with the universe, and all life is ours. We find ourselves immersed with the *"kingdom of God that lies within."* We understand that all is one, and we are one with all life—animate and inanimate—and the universe itself.

The Ego

The ego assures us that we can get along just fine in the limited physical sensibilities that we have in this world. To function in the physical world, the ego has to limit our intake to only those things that we can see, touch, taste, hear, and smell. The ego cannot handle anything outside the physical reality it understands. The biggest block to entering the mystical world of contemplation is the ego. It is the part of the psyche that limits contact with the universe, working to bring us back into the 'real world' of time and the senses. The ego pummels our minds when we are in that suspenseful moment of awe with our newborn child or grandchild, insisting that we return to earth and stay alert since something may happen.

The ego works hard to keep us aware of our senses and the passing of time. The ego chatters at us constantly and is the voice that rolls on and on in our heads. As the years go by, the ego and the sensory world the ego understands tend to dominate more and more of our lives. There is no room for the Eternal Wisdom to speak to us—unless we take the time to develop that internal side of us that is in contact with the universal language of the Eternal Wisdom.

The tools I have spoken of were developed to find a path through the jungle of the ego. We can take those tools, adjust them to fit who we are, and find the road that brings us to the possibility of contemplation. If we are sufficiently open, the Eternal Wisdom may invite you in—if it will benefit you at the time. Achieving or not achieving the level of contemplation spoken of here is a gift that is timed to fit your growth in the path of eternity. It is a great thing to achieve and is never forgotten, but it is not a critical thing to occur. Mother Teresa wrote to her spiritual guide toward the end of her life that she had not had that transcendent experience in fifty years—but look at the love she exhibited in her own way. She did not need the bliss of the contemplative experience to achieve an extraordinary level of love; those of us who have the experience need that experience to move forward.

The Path of Contemplation

When you realize you are in contemplation, you are already on the way out. Contemplation can only be recognized in hindsight. After a contemplative experience, you will

My life is my message.
—Mahatma Gandhi

know, without a doubt, that you were in the zone of contemplation. If you have any doubt, then you were not in contemplation. The experience is that powerful. Most often, it will be only a momentary experience, but since it is a timeless experience, it will be so ingrained in your memory that you will never forget the experience.

From all that I have seen, times of ecstasy come when we are in places of profound peace and quiet, which is why having a place for quiet time is important. We leave room for the Holy Spirit to work with us in the depths of our quiet souls. We can surrender our inner selves unto the Holy Spirit to find peace.

There is a cautionary note. The gift of contemplation is a gift from the Eternal Wisdom. We have no control over the length, depth, or content of the experience. We cannot even choose or not choose to have the experience. What occurs is up to the Holy Spirit— even though the basic form will be extracted from your memories so that it makes some sense to you. Whether it will be an experience in the body or an experience out of the body will depend on your hidden expectations. During the experience, you will probably not know it is occurring.

It always comes when we are not looking for anything so wondrous, and it always catches us by surprise. It never occurs when we expect it to occur, and anytime we try to set a stage where it might occur, it will be like the wind in the willow—just out of reach. If we try to reach for it, it will dance just out of sight— there but not there. Contemplation never comes at our beckoning.

If it is planned for with strategic prayers, wonderful prayer settings, beautiful lights, and glorious places, the experience will be wonderful, but it will not be contemplation. It will be a deep meditation— beautiful but not that heart-stopping pause that true contemplation brings.

What if, despite all that you do, these prayer experiences never occur? That is all right too. These experiences are nice and provide an internal kick that is hard to replace, but they are not required. Mother Teresa did not need them to remain true to her path. She apparently had them when younger, and she missed the experiences, but the memories of them were sufficient to keep her going. The experiences are nice, and you may be blessed to receive them, but their lack of presence does not mean that all your work and prayers are for naught.

Even if we do not experience these moments during our quiet time, we will continue to have them when a sudden sight of awe strikes us in a more natural setting, such as a walk in the woods, a museum where the wonders of art can enthrall us, our family enchanting us, or an infinite number of settings that our Eternal Wisdom opens for us.

The purpose of all that we have talked about, including this discussion of contemplation, is to live a life of abundance, a life filled with joy and happiness. When we have these experiences, it is icing on the cake. They do not make or break us in the quest for abundance. They add to the experience, and life goes on. I want to stress that contemplation is a gift that is meant to encourage us and show us that we are on a path that intersects with God in this world of physicality. God is in all, and in these moments of awe, we have been given the gift to see the wonder of God in everything. Eternal life fills all that we are.

I know a man in Christ who fourteen years ago
Was caught up in the third heaven—
Whether in the body or out of the body,
I don't know, God knows.
—2 Corinthians 12:2, NIV

Questions to Ponder

Where do you practice your quiet time? Do you have a place where you can relax and just let the Holy Spirit speak without being interrupted? Is the cell phone on mute? Is the computer off? You need to assure your subconscious that you will not be disturbed.

Write down how you can assure yourself that you can find a spot of peace in your space and time.

Does your quiet time contain some part where you can be still and hear the small whisper of God leading you forward?

Meditation

Eternal Wisdom, you gift me with moments so profound that the world stops while I gaze in wonder at the sight of heaven within. It always comes as a surprise, and it is all the more wondrous as a surprise. I are thankful when I receive one of these magical moments, long or short. Most of all, I am grateful for the joy and happiness that you bless me with. I know these moments of wonder tell me what the state of transition awaits us so that this life of physicality can contain the same wonder as the life beyond time. Life can be enchanting, and I ask that my hidden mystical eyes continue to expand so that we may see more and more of the wonder of the universe and beyond. You continually grant me peace and joy, and I am grateful for the times I have glimpsed this same peace and joy in my life. I am especially grateful for the wondrous beauty that always is around and in me at all times. I ask for your help in seeing this ever-present kingdom of heaven that is mine to live in always—if we but have eyes to see.

Chapter 38

Living the Life of Abundance

For it is in giving that we receive.
—Prayer of Saint Francis

Saint Francis Sums up Living the Life of Abundance

*W*hen we start to live the life of abundance, life changes. Joy and happiness begin to fill our lives, but we feel restless and that something is missing. Yes, life is becoming joyful and happy, but we can sense that something is lacking to bring the joy we have to fruition. This feeling is correct; something is missing. What is missing is a response to living a life of abundance. We need to find the increasing level of joy that is ours for the taking. Giving of yourself completes the cycle and raises your consciousness to a level of the sublime. We join with the oneness that is who we are, and the fire of divine joy fills our hearts

331

and being. We know we are one with God, the Eternal Wisdom.

This step raises us to the sublime. This is the step that takes us from those who say "Lord, Lord" but do nothing and joins us with the work of the Holy Spirit. Jesus was very blunt about this. *"Many will say to me on that day, 'Lord, Lord, have we not prophesied in thy name? And in thy name have cast out devils? And in thy name done many wonderful works?' And then I will profess to them: I never knew you: depart from me, you that work iniquity"* (Matt. 7:21–23, KJV). These harsh words are aimed at spurring his listeners and understanding that we must do something with the gifts given us.

"What does it profit, my brethren, if someone says he has faith but does not have works? Can faith save him? Thus also faith by itself, if it does not have works, is dead" (James 2:14–17, King James 2000). These are very strong words, but a wonderful thing occurs when we start to walk the road of a life of abundance. Opportunities open before us for sharing our joy and love with others that we did not see before. Perhaps they were there before and we were blind to them, but now that our eyes have been opened, opportunities are presented to us in a manner that we can see.

We begin to understand that we are one—and when we help another, we are helping a part of ourselves. When we fail to help another, we cut ourselves off from the oneness of all. We strangle the budding joy and happiness that should be ours. That is the meaning behind the harsh words of Jesus and the warning of Saint James. We are one. When we try to keep our newfound joy to ourselves and refuse those opportunities presented to us, we are denying our oneness, and we cut ourselves off from the truth of life.

Jesus said, *"Whatever you did to the least of these brothers and sister of mine, you did it to me"* (Matt. 25:40, ESV). Quantum physics says that we are all one and nothing separates us in the reality of physicality or spirituality—but our egos tell us that it isn't so.

The Franciscan mystic Richard Rohr said,

> *"Matter and spirit have always been one, since God decided to manifest God's self in the first act of creation. Modern science, especially quantum physics and biology, is demonstrating that this is the case. Where does this endless drive toward life, multiplication, fecundity, creativity, self-perpetuation, and generativity come from, except from something/someone we call an indwelling Spirit?"*

We are one being—one in spirit and one in being and one in physicality—since everything in the universe is made up of the same quanta material, flowing through and in us.

We can attempt to stay separate, and the ego demands that we stay separate, but the reality is that we are not separate in physical makeup or spiritual being. Biology shows us that, on average, every cell in our bodies is replaced by new and fresh cells every seven years or so (individual cells live from a few hours (the colon) to a lifetime (the brain)), which means that I have gone through, on average, more than eleven 'new bodies' in my lifetime.

When we join our fellow humans in the spirit of giving of ourselves and our material and spiritual goods, we find that we have joined the universe in the care of that universe. We are not alone in spirit or physical being, but our support structure is all tied into one package—both the small blue world we call home and the seven billion souls that exist on that world. When we withhold from giving to that world, we withhold giving to ourselves. We cut off our mental being from that world, isolating the self in the ego. We cut the self off from the source of joy and happiness, wondering why the promise of joy and happiness is eluding us.

Jesus said, "I never knew you. Depart from me."

By our actions, we are known. When we depart from our source, we find ourselves isolated in the ego and fear, missing the wider world of the Spirit that is ours for the taking. We can never miss the ultimate goal of our lives—rejoining the bliss when this journey is over—but we will have failed to reach the goals we set for ourselves when we entered the physical world.

Everything is one thing.

One of the wonders of quantum physics is that in the world of the very small, everything is a bond of something we call energy, but it is different from what we know as electricity or similar bonds. It's a formless field of nothingness and everything. The energy of everything includes the universe as a whole, spreading from the very small to the vastness of the universe. These bonds reach across the stars and maintain the hundreds of billions of stars in the heavens, the galaxies, the super galaxies, the universe, and our planet, the soil under our feet, the hair on our bodies, and our very lives. This energy is alive—moving, shifting, changing at the speed of light—no matter if it is a galaxy, a star, a planet, a rock—or you or me.

The Super Hadron Collider is giving us a peek into the untold energy that fills everything we behold and forms all that we know in the physical world. The oneness of everything, separated only by minute shifts in the energy bonds between everything is life itself. What happens to one thing—no matter where it occurs in the universe—eventually affects everything in the universe to some degree. The closer the energy bonds are, the quicker the effect—and the stronger the effect.

Quantum physics states that everything is moving, no matter what we see. Everything is alive, everything is a form of life, and all life is one action. All life is joined through the bonds of attraction that is the universe itself.

This life energy holds it all together in a single, interrelated form of life that we call the universe and all that is in it. If we are one in life with the universe, we are one in life with everything in our planet. We are one in life with

When God made up this world of ours, God made it long and wide. And meant that it should shelter all, And none should be denied.
—Carrie Jacobs Bond

plants, animals, and other human beings. Anything we do affects all others, and when we do something to another, we do it to ourselves. Two thousand years ago, Jesus said, *"What you do for another, you do to me"* (Matt. 25, NIV).

If we do it for the Jesus in anyone, we do it for ourselves in that same vein. Jesus, like all humanity, is in you and me—in spirit as well as energy. We are all one, as we are one with our planet. The damage we do to the planet we do to ourselves, and the support we give to the planet gives support to ourselves.

Science has determined that all is one, and spiritual teachings the world over have agreed. The flutter of a butterfly in San Francisco affects the atmosphere in India, and quite truthfully, it affects the behavior of the farthest star in the universe.

Somehow, science and spirituality have managed to arrive at the same point. All is one—one Force, one Life, one Being—and we can only sense a tiny, time-limited, infinitely small portion of that Life, which we call God.

The Work Before Us

We are all one being. If we desire to live a life of abundance and find joy and happiness in life, we better align our lives with the energy of life in our universe. To attain a life of abundance, we give a life of abundance. To receive joy, give joy. To receive happiness, we give happiness.

What you give away to others, you give to yourself. It does not matter where you find yourself drawn, you will find opportunities to give in small things like giving to the street person with the cup or pail held out, picking up a piece of rubbish on the street, or giving to organizations or causes you believe in. You could even start an organization that feeds the hungry in your community.

The more you give of time and monies, the more you receive. The Prayer of St Francis says, "For it is in giving that you receive." It is as simple as that. Sometimes our lives only permit us small amounts of time due to family and job situations, but what you do with that time is what counts.

Everyone can give something to someone or something to aid our planet. A poor woman gave a small coin to the temple, but as her only coin, it meant more than the rich person who gave plenty, but only a tiny portion of his riches. Everyone can plant a tree, pick up trash, recycle, or create a small beauty that eases a soul passing by. Most of us can give much more than that—time to visit a sick friend, a lonely person in a hospital or retirement home, or someone housebound. You can join a hospice care group, visit a retirement home, or do other positive things

Another opportunity, especially for a person who has an empty nest, is to join a good cause and work with others to accomplish a great deed. There are great groups looking for volunteers to improve society, feed the hungry, care for the environment, or help animals. I cannot keep track of them. I receive, on average, about eight letters a day asking for help. I cannot help them all, but I pick and choose from those that appeal to me.

What you give to others you give to yourself. If you want joy, be joyful and bring joy to others.

The Golden Rule is of no use whatsoever
Unless you realize that it is your move.
—Dr. Frank Crane

Questions to Ponder

Look at your life over the past twenty-four hours. Where have you been given opportunities to give of yourself to others?

Write down your response to each opportunity and how your response fit your ideal response (or what it could have been).

Meditation

O Comforter, you bring me peace and joy even when things seem unpleasant. I am grateful for your presence. It fills my being, bringing light to the fire of love that seems to overwhelm me at times. I know your love is present, and it is just waiting for my attention to become centered in my life. I am thankful for the ever-expanding sense of life I see in the wonder of nature and the sense of life in the laughter of children and friends you have blessed me with in my life. I thank you for the gift of love that has surrounded me during my life, helping me stay close to your presence despite what was in my life at that moment.

I thank you for the gift of joy, the gift of laughter, and the gift of being able to give where you show me. I ask only for the opportunity to serve you in this life—and to be one with you to see your kingdom on earth that is present around me.

Chapter 39

Why am I not happy?

Joy is the infallible sign of the presence of God.
—Pierre Teilhard de Chardin

Sometimes we think we are doing things in the manner described, but the promises of joy and happiness do not appear. In fact, so much of life stinks. What happened? Why are things like this? I thought these actions would lead me to Easy Street, and everything would be roses.

Working the twelve steps is not just mouthing the words (as thousands of addicts have discovered). It requires commitment to giving your life over to the care of God and taking each day one at a time, working the steps, and taking the time to complete the surrender of self to this higher power.

Once again: Jesus said, *"If anyone says to this mountain, 'Be lifted up and thrown into the sea,' and shall not doubt in his heart, but believes that what he says will happen, it will be granted him"* (Mark 11:23, NASB).

This is the underlying problem. We do not believe God will grant us what we want, and as Jesus indicated, we get what we believe. Our 'wishes' are not granted. The key is to place ourselves totally into the hands of our Eternal Wisdom and surrender into the love that awaits us if we so desire. We are not to *wish* for joy and happiness. We "believe that what we say will happen, and it will be granted." This means an *absolute belief* that our desire for joy and happiness will be granted. This is not faith; it is knowing that it will be granted.

Surrender

It is actually quite simple if you following the simple dictum: "One day at a time." You can drive yourself crazy by thinking, *How am I going to do this every day for the rest of my life?*

All you promise is that today—just today, just this very moment, *now*—I will give my life over to the care of God. One day, one moment, at a time. One prayer, one giving of the day. I will spend today, just today, in surrender to the Eternal Wisdom, and let my worries and concerns rest in the hands of that joy that is inside me all the time ("the kingdom of God lies within"). I *know* that my desire for joy and happiness will be granted, and it shall be.

There are millions of addicts in the world who have gained sobriety from the most grievous addictions that held them in such a grip that it seemed only death could break the spell. These souls who have gained the joy of freedom will tell you cheerfully that it is only done by giving this moment, then the next, and then the next, over to the care of God as they understand God. There is no other way. That is the only road to freedom and joy.

The most difficult part of the process is understanding that the steps are not just words printed on a page. "Oh yes, this is great. All I have to do is this, and all will be well." You can't put it aside like a newspaper. "Ah, yes. I understand. What's next?"

We are so used to throwaway news that we see every day that we flinch when we realize that these approaches to a life of joy requires daily monitoring for the rest of our lives—even though it is "one day at a time." Having something requiring discipline in life is a different mind-set that requires effort to achieve. Most failures to achieve joy and happiness in life are a result of not wanting to apply the discipline it requires. We have become used to instant gratification; with a simple swipe of the credit card, we have the next great thing. It's great—until the next great thing comes along. We are trying to achieve lasting joy and happiness that does not diminish or vanish from one day to the next.

The discipline is not odorous. It becomes one of the greatest joys in life, but daily discipline must be adhered to if the results are to be what we set out to find.

Do we want to find unlimited joy and happiness? Part of the problem is that we have never had unlimited joy and happiness. Even though it kind of sounds good, is it *that* good? All you can do is take the

When you do things from your soul, you feel a river moving in you, a joy.
—Rumi

words and comfort from those who have found joy and happiness—even in times of sorrow, stress, sickness, health, death, or transition. The results are worth everything you have in life. *"Again, the kingdom of heaven is like a merchant seeking beautiful pearls, who, when he had found one pearl of great price, went and sold all that he had and bought it"* (Matt. 13:45–46, DARBY).

The Eternal Wisdom is offering each of us that pearl at a great price. It does require us to sell 'all that we have'. We are required to surrender the ego—that self-centeredness that fills our days—and live new lives. We are tuned in to the throb and pulse of the universe that surrounds us, allowing us to receive the gifts of love that flow abundantly around us and contribute to the flow of love that flows through us. We discover that giving joy produces joy and giving happiness produces happiness. What we give away, we give to ourselves—each time, every time—without fail.

The Process of Surrender

How often do we surrender to the Eternal Wisdom? Once? Once a year? Once a month? The answer is *now*. Every 'now'. If we want to find joy and happiness, we surrender every moment. God will grant us the ability "to cast the mountain into the sea," that mountain of self-doubt and fear that prevents us from total surrender.

Just for a moment, look at your life. Is anything catastrophic happening? Is everything still while you read these words? While catastrophic events do happen, the odds are that right now, in this moment, everything seems fine. The world is not about to end. Maybe tomorrow, but not right now. How do you feel? Are you sad? Are you just a bit happy? Do some hints of joy fill the air? Are children laughing somewhere? Can you feel the joy? Open your heart and feel the joy in your soul.

If you can feel some happiness, contentment, or joy in the air, God has answered your desires. God exists only in the now—never in the past or in the future. Every religious faith teaches this. The only place you will feel the joy and happiness we have been talking about is right now. Only right *now*!

Now

Every 'now' is a new 'now'. Each moment, each nanosecond, is new. It did not exist before it appears, and it will never exist again. And like the quantum field, it has an infinite range of possibilities until the 'now' explodes into being, following on the heels of the previous 'now'. Each 'now' is a new possibility, and it does not have to be linked into the previous 'now'. If we surrender this 'now' into the power within each of us, we can change direction and discover that "the mountain is cast into the sea," just as Jesus said it would. We will discover a sense of joy and happiness that we did not know existed.

That new possibility that exists in this 'now' can be more joyful than the 'now' that just passed because that possibility exists. All we do is will it into existence by letting the kingdom of God within come forth from within our souls.

I cannot stress enough that we have control of how we perceive the world in every moment of our lives. Our perception of the world around us is our own personal universe, and it is the only universe we can know and understand. By changing our perceptions of the smallest events in our lives, we change the direction of the unfolding of our lives—event by event. This changing of perception opens up possibilities that can change the direction of our lives.

Jesus said, *"And shall not doubt in his heart, but believes that what he says will happen, it will be granted him.*" He is talking about a perception of the world—a perception that what was desired to happen would happen because we desired it to happen and nothing more. Doubt cannot enter into the equation. Even the slightest doubt limits the possibility that it can occur. The slightest doubt becomes an instant landslide into failure.

Jesus said, *"If you have the faith like a mustard seed, you would say to this mulberry tree, 'Be uprooted and be planted in the sea,' and it would obey you"* (Luke 17:6, NASB).

Recite to yourself: "I am going to change the way I think about the presence of joy and happiness. I will no longer use the word *desire*. Instead, I will use the word *know*." We will stop saying we desire joy and happiness. Instead, we will say that we *know* we are and will be joyful and happy.

The process is simple, but it requires a shift in our lives in thinking and doing. The following steps will lead you to this level of behavior in a gentle and continuous life:

1. Meditate for at least fifteen minutes every day, preferably in the morning, to set your mind in a good direction for the rest of the day.
2. Stop filling your mind with negative thoughts that have no meaning in your life. Most news is filled with negative information that has no impact now or in the future on your life. Cease following every news story as if it has some

meaning to your life since 99.99 percent (and a lot more nines) of stories have zero impact on any portion of your life. I no longer watch any news broadcasts, but I keep aware of the world events in sufficient depth to understand what others know so I can discuss it if it seems important to them.

3. Find sources of joy to be part of your life. Children are a special source of joy, with their gifts of uninhibited joy and laughter. I find music to be a bringer of joy, and I find sources of that type of music and use it daily. (I use many sources except modern rock. It must be my age! But I really do like Billy Joel.). Each of us has sources of joy that we can draw upon. Make a list of the things that bring you joy—and use those items to fill your days.

4. Read joyful or uplifting stories, poetry, and scriptural texts from many sources—not only Christian sources (or if you are not Christian, do not read only from your religious sources).

5. Help someone in need and feel the joy of giving.

6. Even in bad situations, find something to bring a smile to your face. There is always something to smile about somewhere—a child, a joke, a flower, or something that will give you a moment of joy.

7. Avoid things that upset you and have no meaning in your life.

8. Do good—and avoid that which you know is bad.

9. Look for the good in others. There is always good to be seen if you look.

Following these and similar lists of actions will allow the grace of God to fill your life in a constant rush. It will cause you to wonder how you ever saw life as dull or anxious. It will bring joy and happiness to every moment of your life—until you transition into the next stage of life.

> ***Walk as if you are kissing the earth with your feet.***
> ***—Thich Nhat Hanh***

Questions to Ponder

Look at your day. Write down how you spend the day. Do you do things to reduce stress and keep outward worries to a minimum?

How do you find the joys of life that are placed in your path by God? Do you welcome them and let them fill your soul?

Meditation

Great Spirit, you have made me in your image and likeness, filling me with love and life. I am grateful for all that you have shown me, and I eagerly await the joy that is mine to experience each moment of my life, here and beyond. You have given me this world, which has so much beauty and grace to sustain me. You fill my life with opportunities to dip into that beauty and grace to fill me to overflowing levels of joy and life. You have shown me the beauty of your existence and are constantly offering me ways to find joy to celebrate life in the fullest. I marvel at the green of summer, the blue sky that is filled with the wonders of our universe at night, the warmth that celebrates life, the rainstorms that bring life to my earth and my body, and the beauty of the snow of winter. You let me marvel at diversity and enjoy the wonders of spring. You fill my life with the beauty of my fellow travelers, from the newborn child to the care-worn adult. I am thankful for the ability to see beauty in this world of mine—that wondrous ability to take this chaotic world and see the perfect order that is there. Keep me fresh and green, I ask of you, no matter my age or circumstances.

Chapter 40

Now

True power is within, and it is available now.
—Eckhart Tolle

I explained the concept of *now* as being the key to living in joy and happiness. Have that "faith of a mustard seed" that Jesus spoke about. Having 'no doubt' is required for achieving our desires in life.

Now is a simple word. We all believe we understand what it means. It means right now or in this very instant. Wikipedia says, "Now commonly refers to the present time." Simple enough. So, what is the problem?

Eckhart Tolle's *The Power of Now* described it in far better depth than I can use in these discussions. A unique perception on life arises when we view all of life from the singular perspective of 'now'. I am attempting to give a perspective that can be used to live a life of abundance, that is, a life filled with joy and happiness. I heartily recommend that you read his marvelous book to grasp the breathtaking possibilities that exist when one lives in the constant *now* that is every moment.

I am going to simplify it a bit and concentrate on the task at hand: living a life of abundance. To find joy and happiness in every moment means that we live in *"that kingdom of heaven that lies within."* To live in that kingdom of heaven, we live in the presence of God since that is the definition of heaven. Heaven is the bliss of God—nothing less and nothing more. Living in the bliss of God is, by definition, living a life of joy and happiness.

All the previous discussions about living the twelve steps of abundance are nothing more than a road map for living in the 'now'. They allow us to let the past go into the past and accept the future as it unfolds as a series of events that are not aimed at us personally.

Normal Thought Processing

For most of humanity, the thought process rarely leads from the concept of 'now'. Usually we are immersed in the past or concerned about the future—or both at the same time. We seldom take the time to enjoy the moment, and our thoughts are racing ahead. Watch your next conversation. Do you really listen to the other person? Or are you racing ahead, framing your answer, while the other person is still talking? When we meet someone who actually listens to us, most of us become flustered and find our own thoughts breaking up. "I am actually being heard!" I know of only a very few people who truly listen in conversations. I am guilty of not listening way too often—ok, most of the time.

351

How many times have we planned a day's outing and packed a wonderful meal? When we arrive, we worry about bugs, the possibility of rain or too much sun, not spilling ketchup, and whether we left the water running. When the day is over, we remember very little about the actual

> *Our attention is in the moment. We are not afraid of the future or ashamed of the past.*
> *—Jose Luis Ruiz, The Fifth Agreement*

event. We have missed it! We spent the afternoon worrying about a potential future (which seldom happens) or the past. We missed the joys of time with family and friends. We seldom pause to enjoy the moment, that moment where we let everything else go out of our minds just to enjoy the 'now'.

Our failure to see the 'now' in each moment is the reason we are stunned when something catches us off guard, like a beautiful sunset. It grabs us and makes us speechless. It becomes an event that we remember long after the occurrence, but the picnic with family and friends becomes a blur in our memory and is forgotten—except for a photo or two to remind us.

Life is only in this very moment. Life does not exist outside of this moment. When we spend our time worrying about the future and mulling over the past, we miss the moment that is going on right 'now'. Too many of us dwell on past slights or damages or worrying about some future event that we miss the present.

The Past

We worried about the past like a dog chewing on an old bone, hoping to find something new. Somebody said or did something to us, and we proceed to chew on it, turning it into a monster that eats us alive. It is true that something was done to us, perhaps something terrible, but does constantly thinking about it change anything? It is true that something that occurs in our lives can have far-reaching effects and can change our lives significantly, but what has happened has happened. Nothing we say or think about it will change the event. It is finished, already written in the sands of the past.

Think of the worst thing that can happen to you. Your spouse left you. An accident left you paralyzed. A fire destroyed everything you own. Events like these require strict discipline of the mind to control the screaming thoughts that occur, but none of the thoughts help the situation. Sit down and review the present position—perhaps on paper or at least in the mind. Recognize that so-and-so occurred, and accept the fact as real, and then take the next step to recover.

The event that occurred is usually not catastrophic. It is just something we find irritating at the very least. All the chewing on the event will not change what occurred. When we are irritated about something that someone did, that person may have no idea that he or she offended you. He or she has forgotten it as soon as it happened, and the person remains oblivious to the anger you feel.

All your fuming accomplishes nothing except causing you to waste time, and we only have our allotted time and no more. When we waste time in this fashion, we fail to meet our objective in our lives for this period of our existence. In fact, this type of fuming sets events that force us to recover just to be back where we were (in the metaphysical realm).

When we spend time in the past, we miss the 'now'. The present event is the only place where we can find the love of God. The universe that we see ourselves existing in is a product of our past. Things only make sense based on the events that occurred in the past. We are to be especially prudent to limit our use of the past to only that portion that permits us to understand the world we are in. We know what a tree is because we have been told that these objects with thick brown things rising into the air from the ground, with smaller versions of the thick thing going off to the sides, with perhaps these green soft things attached, is called a tree. We have been told often enough, and we see it is accepted by others, that we also call it a tree. Using this form of prior knowledge is the correct way to use the past.

Any other use of the past will not find the joy and happiness of God. God does not live in the past. God is the very essence of 'now'. If you want to join in that essence of joy, you keep your awareness on the now as it unfolds in your life from moment to moment.

Eckhart Tolle said, *"Nothing ever happened in the past that can prevent you from being present now; and if the past cannot prevent you from being present now, what power does it have?"*

The Future

To use the past to grow fearful scenarios about the future is the wrong way to use it. Our imaginations, especially when we are under stress, revert back to using the reptilian brain (the fight-or-flight brain). We then encourage our brains in that mode of existence, feeding more imaginative thoughts that amplify the potential horrors that crowd the mind, freeze our consciousness, lock out our souls, raise our blood pressure, and take over our bodies.

Like Chicken Little, we yell, "The world is ending. The world is ending!" We panic. I know too many people who are in a panic over illegal immigrants—even though they do not know any illegal immigrants. They usually have never had any contact with any illegal immigrants. But the illegal immigrant is the image of God and is indeed a unique face of God. The complainers have eaten the lettuce that the illegal immigrant picked—and enjoyed other results of these hidden and unwanted jobs that the illegal immigrants perform—but pointing out all the effort and work that these people do makes no dent in their fear or anxiety. They imagine that all the illegal immigrants want is to rape and pillage, fed by Fox News and its copycats, and are buried in their fears.

Imagination is a wonderful gift from God, and it is the basis of all the wonderful advances we have made in medicine and technology. We often use this gift to hide from the present moment. We spend so much of our time worrying about the what-ifs that we forget to see the wonders that God hands to us each day. We worry that our income will vanish. Did it vanish today? If not, accept that fact and move on with life.

Every time a worry comes up, ask if there is anything you can do at that moment to ease the situation should it arise. If the answer is yes, then do it. If the answer is no, then let it go. In either case, further worrying will not change the situation. If it happens, you have done all you could to ease the situation. If it doesn't happen—and more than 99 percent of the time it won't—all that worrying did was reduce your health and shorten your life span.

One of the secrets to finding joy and happiness in this life is living with each moment, tasting each moment, sensing each moment where you are, and just letting it be. God is present in everything and everywhere in the universe, including the time and space where you are right now.

The twelve steps open you up to the presence of God in the here and now—right now! Not yesterday and not tomorrow, but now. God is present in each and every 'now', no matter what the circumstances, wonderful or horrifying. God is present everywhere and in everything, and God *is* everything and *fills* everything. There is no location where God is not, from the infinitely small to the infinitely large, from the quantum wave to the universe and beyond.

> ***Now is all there is, the only time that is real.***
> ***Cherish it.***
> ***Dwell on the beauty of life.***
> ***Watch the stars,***
> ***And see yourself running with them.***
> ***—Marcus Aurelius***

Questions to Ponder

Do you find yourself worrying about the past and worrying about the future? Keep a record of how much time you chew on the past and worry about the future in a single day.

What can you do to reduce this wasted time? Could this be the time you need for quiet time?

Meditation

My Wondrous One, I am grateful for the life you have granted me, for the beauty of this marvelous moment, and for the song of 'now'. I understand that you are only 'now', and I create my present situation by my perception of 'now'—each and every moment. I marvel at the beauty of life that surrounds me at every moment. The song of the birds, the glitter of snow, the glory of the night sky, the smell of newly mown grass, and the beauty of the flower are gifts from your bounty and fill our days with glory. You have shown me by all these glories that I can fill my awareness only in the 'now', that glorious 'now'. Only in this 'now' can I see your glory and taste your wonder of life, knowing that only by seeing it *now* can I see it more gloriously in the next 'now'.

I stand in awe at life that flows around me. I see your glow in the faces of all I meet. I see your beauty in the stranger in the street—stranger no more as the face of God shines back at me. I marvel in the vitality of life that seems to blaze forth from every corner of the earth—from the smallest microbe to the elephant that trumpets your glory. I give glory for all that is mine to behold, and I bow in gratitude for the gift of heaven on earth, as you promised from the beginning.

Chapter 41

Conclusion

For behold, the kingdom of God is within.
—Luke 17:21

This quote from Luke spells out the essence of what we are to know as we face God, the essence of the universe. God exists everywhere and in everything, but God is most accessible within us. The purpose of the practice of quiet time is to access our innermost being where the seemingly elusive "kingdom of God" resides.

We have looked at a process to find joy and happiness in our lives, irrespective of what is occurring in our lives, good or not so good. I have used a process of unfolding the interior drive that leads us forward in life, finding and living in that "kingdom that dwells within," as promised by Jesus and spoken by all the prophets of all religions and faiths.

My life has revealed a remarkable truth. If you maintain the deep knowledge that God will always provide the way to a life of joy and happiness, despite all that you have done in life, that energy level of joy will always be present—even when you are dwelling in depression that seems impossible to exit. As my life progressed, I realized this powerful truth to be a living reality, and I have attempted to share how this miracle occurred.

Sixty years ago, I did not understand or even expect that my life would be filled with joy no matter what I did. As I began to analyze my life in my seventies, I realized that I had stumbled upon one of the true miracles of life. Life can be joyful under all conditions, and the conditions will shift to give this blazing glory of life the best possible opportunities to be a wondrous journey that is available to us under any and all circumstances.

The path is not arduous. In fact, it provides a path to joy under all circumstances. It does require a level of commitment, day after day, under all trials and tribulations, as well as under all levels of joy and happiness. I have discovered, much to my amazement, that it is more difficult to follow the path when everything is going well than when everything seems to be falling apart. Perhaps disaster always seems to be lurking around the corner so that I won't become complacent.

When we are falling apart, we seek help in all forms. When we have found something that helps, we turn back to that aid when ill. However, when things are going well, we are like seriously ill people who stop taking medication because they are feeling better. When we stop taking our spiritual medicine, we will find ourselves back in the humdrum frenzy of everyday life or sliding into depression or whatever it was. We will have lost that sense of the presence of the universe that is always smiling at us, offering joy at any time we accept it.

The Path

The path is following the way of the twelve steps as outlined. These steps are a gift from God. Nothing lies outside the realm of the Being we call God, and nothing exists but within that realm. God provides a path to the kingdom of God within, and that path can only be found by going within. By going into the spirit in periods of quiet time, we reach the within, where the kingdom of God resides.

This path is only one of myriad paths that can be found to reach that kingdom of God within, but it is a sure path for those willing to venture along to eternity. We are called into this path; it is a path into eternity. Joys beyond measure await us for the acceptance of that world that is just beyond the physical realm.

You may have noted that I was careful not to state that only these prayers in this or that manner will provide the way. Each of us must find his or her own path to reach eternity. I have given many hints and suggestions, all of which have worked for me at one time or another, but no one way will work for all.

Certainly no one way will work all the time, but one way will work for you right now. That way will probably change many times over a lifetime. The secret is to not be overcome by the way this or that path does not work or ceases to work. Just find another path.

The Starting Path

The starting path is easy. Read one meditation from this book per day—and act on it. Follow the suggested Questions to Ponder and see where they lead you. This forty-day path will begin to instill that daily habit of quiet time in your life. Allow it to become something that will occur each day. The key is to form a habit of daily quiet time so that it will become one of the cornerstones of your daily life.

Keep a record of your daily practice. This helps reduce the days that you skip. It will remind you of your daily venture and reward you with the acknowledgement that you have succeeded in meeting your internal commitment to a daily practice period.

If you find it expedient, read these meditations as many times as they support your practice. I have often gone back to readings and resources that have proven helpful to me in the past, and they again prove helpful in my journey.

Do not expect long periods of joy and happiness in the beginning. They tend to sneak up on you, surprising you at unexpected moments. These happen in their own time and are a gift from God for your adventure to the life within. You will find joy in the success rate you have in your journal, but that is only a start.

The day will come when you will wake up filled with the joy of being alive. You will wake up to life in a fresh new day, the greatest gift of all. You will realize that things have gone amazingly well—even when things have gone in strange ways. To others, it may seem bad, but it still worked out better than if it had gone on an apparent *better* path. Life can be good—no matter what is occurring.

Friends and family will have tragedies and really bad events, but soon you will understand, in your heart, that these events will lead only to a more positive outcome for them—even when they transition from the physical world. After all, we know that death cannot occur, and all life continues, no matter what it seems.

The Long Haul

The path outlined is the path I have used for more than sixty years. It could stretch for almost eighty years since I roamed the fields and forests around my home in rural Ohio as a small child of four. For hours, I imagined that my friend Jesus was with me. He was a small child too, and we carried on long conversations. Jesus was my invisible friend, and we talked often (which worried my mother). I spent most of my time alone outside, as there were no other small children around. Just God and I.

I have learned that we each walk our own paths, led by the interior spirit where the kingdom of God resides. Do not be afraid to venture off into any approach that brings you peace, joy, and happiness. Your spirit knows what is ideal for you at this moment of physicality.

The venture continues each day, and the days pile up. They become years and then decades; before you know it, a lifetime of dwelling in the peace of God goes by, much to the delight of your soul and to the delight of all you cross paths with along the way. Your aura of the love of God will spill out and entice all who know you—even though most will not recognize what draws them to you.

Acknowledgments

My life has been filled with gifts of wisdom that have somehow found their way through my thick skull (at least partially). I have been the recipient of untoward wisdom, some of which stuck, that has dramatically changed my life's direction and purpose.

My parents, Pete and Katie, gave me the freedom from a very young age to find God in the wonders of the woods and farmlands of our small home in the middle of north-central Ohio. They shared the gentle wisdom of their love of nature and God and their fierce fight against racial injustice during a time when such injustice was not even thought about.

My brother Tom showed me the love of God as he went through his life of service to humanity despite all the obstacles thrown into his life. He never lost his sense of humor or his love of God. He brought me back to my faith in my teen years, and he inspired me all of my life with his love of service.

To the many masters who were brought into my life at times when I was ready for that given teacher. (The teacher will appear when the student is ready). Father Jim Brown taught me the value of prayer. Irmis Popoff showed me the wisdom of being "awake." The Cursillo Movement gave me the understanding of true leadership and service that are the hallmarks of the God person. Gurdjieff and Ouspensky taught me the wisdom and methods of rising to the fourth way. Tom Powers taught me the power of living the twelve steps.

So many others whose lives have crossed mine in breathtaking synchronicity. Neale Donald Walsch's Conversations with God series gave written documentation to all that I had deduced over the years.

As the focus of the dedication of this effort, my wife Eileen—my sure guide through the challenges that have faced me over the past fifty-seven years—never failed to give me her love through it all. Her love has been my guide and my signpost of the love of God when things have been difficult.

I can be reached through my website, www.davidlendonpeters.com. I welcome comments and discussions on this book or on my blogs. I write meditative blogs once or twice a week on various topics.